LANGUAGE DEATH

DAVID CRYSTAL

CAMBRIDGE
UNIVERSITY PRESS

CAMBRIDGE
UNIVERSITY PRESS

University Printing House, Cambridge CB2 8BS, United Kingdom

One Liberty Plaza, 20th Floor, New York, NY 10006, USA

477 Williamstown Road, Port Melbourne, VIC 3207, Australia

4843/24, 2nd Floor, Ansari Road, Daryaganj, Delhi - 110002, India

79 Anson Road, #06-04/06, Singapore 079906

Cambridge University Press is part of the University of Cambridge.

It furthers the University's mission by disseminating knowledge in the pursuit of education, learning and research at the highest international levels of excellence.

www.cambridge.org
Information on this title: www.cambridge.org/9781107431812

© David Crystal 2000, 2014

First published 2000
Reprinted 2000
Canto edition 2002
Ninth printing 2010
Canto Classics edition 2017

A catalogue record for this publication is available from the British Library

ISBN 978-1-107-43181-2 Paperback

CONTENTS

PREFACE

In 1992, linguists attending the International Linguistics Congress in Quebec agreed the following statement:

As the disappearance of any one language constitutes an irretrievable loss to mankind, it is for UNESCO a task of great urgency to respond to this situation by promoting and, if possible, sponsoring programs of linguistic organizations for the description in the form of grammars, dictionaries and texts, including the recording of oral literatures, of hitherto unstudied or inadequately documented endangered and dying languages.

UNESCO did respond. At a conference in November 1993, the General Assembly adopted the 'Endangered Languages Project' – including the 'Red Book of Endangered Languages' – and a few months later a progress report observed:

Although its exact scope is not yet known, it is certain that the extinction of languages is progressing rapidly in many parts of the world, and it is of the highest importance that the linguistic profession realize that it has to step up its descriptive efforts.

Several significant events quickly followed. In 1995 an International Clearing House for Endangered Languages was inaugurated at the University of Tokyo. The same year, an Endangered Language Fund was instituted in the USA. The opening statement by the Fund's committee pulled no punches:

Languages have died off throughout history, but never have we faced the massive extinction that is threatening the world right now. As language professionals, we are faced with a stark reality: Much of what we study will not be available to future generations. The cultural heritage of many peoples is crumbling while we look on. Are we willing to shoulder the blame for having stood by and done nothing?

Also in 1995, the Foundation for Endangered Languages was established in the UK. Its second newsletter, summarizing the likely prospects, provides an informal estimate of the scale of the problem:

There is agreement among linguists who have considered the situation that over half of the world's languages are moribund, i.e. not effectively being passed on to the next generation. We and our children, then, are living at the point in human history where, within perhaps two generations, most languages in the world will die out.

Something truly significant is evidently taking place. There has never, in my recollection, been such a universal upsurge of professional linguistic concern. But although the facts, and the reasons behind the facts, are now tolerably clear, most members of the educated public – a public that is usually concerned and vociferous about language and ecology – is still unaware that the world is facing a linguistic crisis of unprecedented scale.

Some people can't or won't believe it. I recall, in early 1997, writing a piece for the *Guardian* about my (at the time) forthcoming book, *English as a global language*. It was a retrospective account of the factors which had promoted the growth of English around the world. At the end of the 2000-word piece, I added a sentence as a speculative teaser. Imagine, I said, what could happen if English continues to grow as it has. Maybe one day it will be the only language left to learn. If that happens, I concluded, it will be the greatest intellectual disaster that the planet has ever known.

The point was incidental, but for many readers it was as if I had never written the rest of the article. The paper's editor made it the keynote of his summary, and most of the published letters which followed focused on the issue of language death. It was good to see so many people being alert and concerned. But the main reaction, in the form of a follow-up article by a journalist the next week, was not so good. He dismissed out of hand the thought that languages could be in danger on a global scale. He had just returned from a visit to Africa, and was filled with pleasurable recollections of the multilingualism he had encountered there; so he concluded that the languages of the world are safe, and that 'a monoglot millennium will never come'.

It was at that point I decided it was essential to write this book – a complementary volume, in some ways, to *English as a global language*. The need for information about language loss is urgent. As the quotations from the various professional groups suggest, we are at a critical point in human linguistic history, and most people don't know.

Language death is real. Does it matter? Should we care? This book argues that it does, and we should. It aims to establish the facts, insofar as they are known, and then to explain them: what is language death, exactly? which languages are dying? why do languages die? – and why apparently now, in particular? It addresses three difficult questions. Why is the death of a language so important? Can anything be done? Should anything be done? The last two questions are especially difficult to answer, and need careful and sensitive debate, but, in this author's mind, the ultimate answers have to be a resounding YES and YES. The plight of the world's endangered languages should be at the top of any environmental linguistic agenda. It is time to promote the new ecolinguistics – to echo an ancient saying, one which is full of colourful and wide-awake green ideas (see pp. 41–2). It needs to be promoted urgently, furiously, because languages are dying as I write. Everyone should be concerned, because it is everyone's loss. And this book has been written to help foster the awareness without which universal concern cannot grow.

The book would have been written in 1997, if I had not been sidetracked by a different but related project, which eventually achieved literary life in the form of a play, *Living on*, which tried to capture imaginatively some of the emotional issues, for both linguists and last speakers, surrounding the topic of language death. Whether a dramatic as opposed to a scholarly encounter with the topic is likely to have greater impact I cannot say. All I know is that the issue is now so challenging in its unprecedented enormity that we need all hands – scholars, journalists, politicians, fund-raisers, artists, actors, directors ... – if public consciousness (let alone conscience) is to be raised sufficiently to enable something fruitful to be done. It is already too late for hundreds of languages. For the rest, the time is now.

It will be obvious, from the frequency of quotations and references in this book, that I have been hugely dependent on the small army of fieldworkers who are actively involved in the task of language preservation around the world. Enough material has now been published to provide the array of examples and illustrations which are needed to put flesh on a general exposition. I have also had the opportunity, in recent travels, to discuss these matters with several of the researchers who are routinely 'out there'. And I have immensely benefited from the comments on a draft of this book provided by Peter Trudgill, Carl James, and Jean Aitchison. Without all these supports, I could not have contemplated writing an overview of this kind; and that is why I have made copious use of the footnote convention, to give due acknowledgement to the crucial role of those who are doing the real work. I hope I have done them no disservice. Although I have never personally spent more than a few hours at a time with endangered language communities abroad, I have used up a good deal of my life working for the maintenance of Welsh at home, and would like to think that I have developed, both intellectually and emotionally, a real sense of the issues.

David Crystal
Holyhead

I

What is language death?

~

The phrase 'language death' sounds as stark and final as any other in which that word makes its unwelcome appearance. And it has similar implications and resonances. To say that a language is dead is like saying that a person is dead. It could be no other way – for languages have no existence without people.

A language dies when nobody speaks it any more. For native speakers of the language in which this book is written, or any other thriving language, it is difficult to envision such a possibility. But the reality is easy to illustrate. Take this instance, reported by Bruce Connell in the pages of the newsletter of the UK Foundation for Endangered Languages (FEL), under the heading 'Obituaries':[1]

During fieldwork in the Mambila region of Cameroon's Adamawa province in 1994–95, I came across a number of moribund languages ... For one of these languages, Kasabe (called Luo by speakers of neighbouring languages and in my earlier reports), only one remaining speaker, Bogon, was found. (He himself knew of no others.) In November 1996 I returned to the Mambila region, with part of my agenda being to collect

---

[1] Connell (1977: 27). The newsletters of this organization changed their name in early issues. The name was *Iatiku* for Numbers 2–4, and *Ogmios* for No. 6 on. Issues 1 and 5 had no distinctive name, and in this book these are referred to as *FEL Newsletter*.

further data on Kasabe. Bogon, however, died on 5th Nov. 1995, taking Kasabe with him. He is survived by a sister, who reportedly could understand Kasabe but not speak it, and several children and grandchildren, none of whom know the language.

There we have it, simply reported, as we might find in any obituary column. And the reality is unequivocal. On 4 November 1995, Kasabe existed; on 5 November, it did not.

Here is another story, reported at the Second FEL Conference in Edinburgh in 1998 by Ole Stig Andersen.[2] This time, 8 October 1992 is the critical day:

The West Caucasian language Ubuh ... died at daybreak, October 8th 1992, when the Last Speaker, Tevfik Esenç, passed away. I happened to arrive in his village that very same day, without appointment, to interview this famous Last Speaker, only to learn that he had died just a couple of hours earlier. He was buried later the same day.

In actual fact, Kasabe and Ubykh (a widely used alternative spelling) had effectively died long before Bogon and Tevfik Esenç passed away. If you are the last speaker of a language, your language – viewed as a tool of communication – is already dead. For a language is really alive only as long as there is someone to speak it to. When you are the only one left, your knowledge of your language is like a repository, or archive, of your people's spoken linguistic past. If the language has never been written down, or recorded on tape – and there are still many which have not – it is all there is. But, unlike the normal idea of an archive, which continues to exist long

---

[2] Andersen (1998: 3).

after the archivist is dead, the moment the last speaker of an unwritten or unrecorded language dies, the archive disappears for ever. When a language dies which has never been recorded in some way, it is as if it has never been.[3]

The language pool

How many languages are at the point of death? How many are endangered? Before we can arrive at an estimate of the scale of the problem, we need to develop a sense of perspective. Widely quoted figures about the percentage of languages dying only begin to make sense if they can be related to a reliable figure about the total number of languages alive in the world today. So how many languages are there? Most reference books published since the 1980s give a figure of between 6,000 and 7,000, but estimates have varied in recent decades between 3,000 and 10,000. It is important to understand the reasons for such enormous variation.

The most obvious reason is an empirical one. Until the second half of the twentieth century, there had been few

---

[3] There is, of course, always the possibility that other speakers of the same dialect will be found. In the Ubykh case, for instance, there were at the time rumours of two or three other speakers in other villages. Such rumours are sometimes found to be valid; often they are false, with the speakers being found to use a different dialect or language. But even if true, the existence of a further speaker or two usually only postpones the real obituary by a short time. For some Aboriginal Australian examples, see Wurm (1998: 193). Evans (forthcoming) provides an excellent account of the social and linguistic issues which arise when working with last speakers, and especially of the problem of deciding who actually counts as being a 'last speaker'.

surveys of any breadth, and the estimates which were around previously were based largely on guesswork, and were usually far too low. William Dwight Whitney, plucking a figure out of the air for a lecture in 1874, suggested 1,000.[4] One language popularizer, Frederick Bodmer, proposed 1,500; another, Mario Pei, opted for 2,796.[5] Most early twentieth-century linguists avoided putting any figure at all on it. One of the exceptions, Joshua Whatmough, writing in 1956, thought there were 3,000.[6] As a result, without professional guidance, figures in popular estimation see-sawed wildly, from several hundred to tens of thousands. It took some time for systematic surveys to be established. *Ethnologue*, the largest present-day survey, first attempted a world-wide review only in 1974, an edition containing 5,687 languages.[7] The Voegelins' survey, published in 1977, included around 4,500 living languages.[8] Since the 1980s, the situation has changed dramatically, with the improvement of information-gathering techniques. The thirteenth edition of *Ethnologue* (1996) contains 6,703 language headings, and about 6,300 living languages are classified in the *International encyclopedia of linguistics* (1992).[9] There

[4] See Silverstein (1971: 113).
[5] Bodmer (1944:405). Pei (1952: 285); in a later book (1954: 127), this total decreased by 1.
[6] Whatmough (1956: 51).
[7] See now the 13th edition, Grimes (1996); also www.sil.org/ethnologue. The first edition in fact dates from 1951, when Richard S. Pittman produced a mimeographed issue of ten pages, based on interviews with people attending the Summer Institute of Linguistics.
[8] Voegelin and Voegelin (1977). I used their total in the first (1987) edition of my *Cambridge encyclopedia of language* (Crystal 1997a).
[9] Bright (1992); the files of *Ethnologue* (then in its 11th edition) were made available for this project, hence the similarity between the totals.

are 6,796 names listed in the index to the *Atlas of the world's languages*.[10] The off-the-cuff figure most often heard these days is 6,000, with the variance sometimes going below, sometimes above.[11] An exceptionally high estimate is referred to below.

A second reason for the uncertainty is that commentators know that these surveys are incomplete, and compensate for the lack of hard facts – sometimes by overestimating, sometimes by underestimating. The issue of language loss is itself a source of confusion. People may be aware that languages are dying, but have no idea at what rate. Depending on how they estimate that rate, so their current global guess will be affected: some take a conservative view about the matter; some are radical. (The point is considered further below.) Then there is the opposite situation – the fact that not all languages on earth have yet been 'discovered', thus allowing an element of growth into the situation. The ongoing exploration of a country's interior is not likely to produce many fresh encounters, of course, given the rate at which interiors have already been opened up by developers in recent years; but in such regions as the islands of Indonesia and

---

[10] This is my count of Mosely and Asher (1994).
[11] Dixon (1997: 143) cites 5,000–6,000, as do Grenoble and Whaley (1998a), in their preface; Wardhaugh (1987: 1) cites 4,000–8,000, and settles on 5,000; Ruhlen (1987) goes for 5,000; Wurm (1991: 1) says 'well over 5,000'; Krauss consulted a number of linguists in writing his article on 'The world's languages in crisis' (1992: 5), and found widespread agreement that 6,000 was a reasonable estimate; Crystal (1997a: 287) also cites 6,000. Other major surveys are in progress: a 'World Languages Report', supported by UNESCO and Linguapax, and financed by the Basque Country, is scheduled for publication in 2001; see also the Global Language Register below.

Papua New Guinea, or the South American or Central African rainforests, reports do come in from time to time of a previously unknown community and language.[12] For example, in June 1998 two such nomadic tribes (the Vahudate and the Aukedate, comprising 20 and 33 families, respectively) were found living near the Mamberamo River area, 2,400 miles east of Jakarta in Irian Jaya. This is a part of the world where the high mountains and deep valleys can easily hide a community, and it is likely that their speech will be sufficiently different from that of other groups to count as a new language. The social affairs office in the region in fact reports that its field officers encounter new groups almost every year.[13]

Even in parts of the world which have been explored, however, a proper linguistic survey may not have been carried out. As many as half the languages of the world are in this position. Of the 6,703 languages listed in the thirteenth edition of *Ethnologue*, 3,074 have the appended comment – 'survey needed'. And what a survey chiefly does is determine whether the speakers found in a given region do indeed all use the same language, or whether there are differences between them. If the latter, it then tries to decide whether these differences amount only to dialect variations, or whether they are sufficiently great to

---

[12] The world's languages have a highly uneven distribution: c. 4% are in Europe; c. 15% in the Americas; c. 31% in Africa; c. 50% in Asia and the Pacific. The countries mentioned have the highest distributions: Papua New Guinea and Indonesia alone have 25% (1,529 languages) between them (according to the 1996 edition of *Ethnologue*).

[13] The report is reproduced in *Ogmios* 9. 6. For similar discoveries in South America, see Adelaar (1998: 12); Kaufman (1994: 47) reports that about 40 languages have been discovered in South America during the past century.

justify assigning the speakers to different languages. Sometimes, a brief preliminary visit assigns everybody to a single language, and an in-depth follow-up survey shows that this was wrong, with several languages spoken. Sometimes, the opposite happens: the initial visit focuses on differences between speakers which turn out not to be so important. In the first case, the number of languages goes up; in the second case, it goes down. When decisions of this kind are being made all over the world, the effect on language counts can be quite marked.

To put some flesh on these statistics, let us take just one of those languages where it is said a survey is needed: Tapshin, according to *Ethnologue* also called Tapshinawa, Suru, and Myet, a language spoken by 'a few' in the Kadun district of Plateau State, Nigeria. It is said to be unclassified within the Benue-Congo broad grouping of languages. Roger Blench, of the Overseas Development Institute in London, visited the community in March 1998, and sent in a short report to the Foundation for Endangered Languages.[14] He stressed the difficulty of reaching the settlement: Tapshin village is a widely dispersed settlement about 25 km north of the Pankshin-Amper road, reached by a track which can be traversed only by a four-wheel drive, and which is often closed during the rainy season. The Tapshin people call themselves Ns'r, and from this derives Blench's name for them, Nsur, and presumably also the name Suru in *Ethnologue*; but they are called Dishili by the Ngas people (referred to as the Angas in *Ethnologue*). The name Myet derives from a settlement, Met, some distance west of Tapshin.

---

[14] Blench (1998).

The Tapshin people claim that the Met people speak 'the same' language as they do, but Blench is cautious about taking this information at face value (for such judgements may be no more than a reflection of some kind of social or historical relationship between the communities). No data seems previously to have been recorded on Nsur. From his initial wordlists, he concludes that there has been substantial mutual influence with the Ngas language. He estimates that there are some 3–4,000 speakers, though that total depends on whether Met is included along with Nsur or not.

This small example illustrates something of the problem facing the linguistic analyst. There is a confusion of names which must be sorted out, in addition to the observable similarities and differences between the speakers.[15] The Nsur situation seems fairly manageable, with just a few alternatives to be considered. Often, the problem of names is much greater. Another Plateau State language, listed as *Berom* in *Ethnologue*, has 12 alternative names: *Birom, Berum, Gbang, Kibo, Kibbo, Kibbun, Kibyen, Aboro, Boro-Aboro, Afango, Chenberom,* and *Shosho*. The task then is to establish whether these are alternative names for the same entity, or whether they refer to different entities – the name of the people, the name of an individual speaker, or the name of the language as known by its speakers (a European analogy would be *Irish, Irishman/woman,* and *Gaelic/Irish/Erse*, respectively). Then there is the question of what the language is called by outsiders. There could of course be several 'outsider'

---

[15] For a discussion of the problem of naming, with particular reference to China, see Bradley (1998: 56 ff.).

names (*exonyms*), depending on how many other groups the language is in contact with (cf. *deutsch* being equivalent to *allemand*, *German*, *Tedesco*, etc.), and these might range from friendly names through neutral names to offensive names (cf. 'He speaks French' vs 'He speaks Frog'). Shosho, in the above list, is apparently an offensive name. But all this has to be discovered by the investigator. There is no way of knowing in advance how many or what kind of answers will be given to the question 'What is the name of your language?', or whether a list of names such as the above represents 1, 2, 6, or 12 languages. And the scale of this problem must be appreciated: the 6,703 language headings in the *Ethnologue* index generate as many as 39,304 different names.

Many of these names, of course, will refer to the dialects of a language. But this distinction raises a different type of difficulty: does a name refer to the whole of a language or to a dialect? The question of whether two speech systems should be considered as separate languages or as dialects of the same language has been a focus of discussion within linguistics for over a century. It is crucial to have criteria for deciding the question, as the decisions made can have major repercussions, when it comes to language counting. Take, for example, the Global Language Register (GLR), in the process of compilation by the Observatoire Linguistique:[16] in a 1997 formulation by David Dalby, this project proposed a threefold nomenclature – of *tongue*

---

[16] The following details are taken from a Logosphere Workshop held at the School of Oriental and African Studies, London, September 1997, specifically from Dalby (1997), and his follow-up paper subsequently circulated.

(or *outer language*), *language* (or *inner language* – or *idiom*, in a further proposal), and *dialect* – to avoid what it considered to be the oversimplified dichotomy of *language* and *dialect*. Early reports related to this project suggested that, using these criteria, an order of magnitude of 10,000 languages was to be expected – a surprisingly large total, when compared with the totals suggested above. The explanation is all to do with methodology. The GLR total is derived from the *tongues* and *idioms* of their system, and includes as languages many varieties which other approaches would consider to be dialects. One example will illustrate the 'inflationary' effect of this approach. The orthodox approach to modern Welsh is to consider it as a single language, with the notable differences between (in particular) north and south Welsh referred to as dialects. On grounds of mutual intelligibility and sociolinguistic identity (of Wales as a nation-principality), this approach seems plausible. The GLR analysis, however, treats the differences between north and south Welsh as justifying the recognition of different languages (each with their own dialects), and makes further distinctions between Old Welsh, Book Welsh, Bible Welsh, Literary Welsh, Modern Standard Welsh, and Learners' Normalized Welsh (a pedagogical model of the 1960s known as 'Cymraeg Byw'). Excluding Old Welsh, in their terms a total of six 'inner languages' can be recognized within the 'outer language' known as modern Welsh. One can see immediately how, when similar cases are taken into account around the world, an overall figure of 10,000 could be achieved.

The language/dialect issue has been addressed so many times, in the linguistics literature, that it would be

gratuitous to treat it in any detail here.[17] In brief, on purely
linguistic grounds, two speech systems are considered to be
dialects of the same language if they are (predominantly)
mutually intelligible. This makes *Cockney* and *Scouse* dialects of English, and *Quechua* a cover-name for over a
dozen languages. On the other hand, purely linguistic
considerations can be 'outranked' by sociopolitical criteria,
so that we often encounter speech systems which are
mutually intelligible, but which have nonetheless been
designated as separate languages. A well-recognized
example is the status of Swedish, Danish, and Norwegian,
which are counted as separate languages despite the fact
that the members of these communities can understand
each other to an appreciable extent. A more recent example
is *Serbo-Croatian*, formerly widely used as a language name
to encompass a set of varieties used within former Yugo-
slavia, but following the civil wars of the 1990s now largely
replaced by the names *Serbian*, *Croatian*, and *Bosnian*. In
1990 there was a single language spoken in these countries;
now there are three. The linguistic features involved have
changed hardly at all; but the sociopolitical situation has
changed irreversibly.

It is of course likely that the linguistic differences
between these languages will increase, as their respective
communities strive to maximize them as symbols of local
identity. This process is already happening. If it continues, then one day it is conceivable that Serbian and
Croatian could become mutually unintelligible – a further
example of something that has happened repeatedly and

---

[17] Standard accounts are to be found in Chambers and Trudgill (1980:
ch. 1) and Crystal (1997a: ch. 47).

normally in linguistic evolution. Indeed, it is possible that a significant increase in the world's languages may one day emerge as an evolutionary consequence of the contemporary trend to recognize ethnic identities. Even global languages could be affected in this way. The point has been noted most often in relation to English, where new varieties have begun to appear around the world, as a consequence of that language's emerging status as a world lingua franca. Although at present Singaporean, Ghanaian, Caribbean, and other 'New Englishes' continue to be seen as 'varieties of English', it is certainly possible for local sociopolitical movements to emerge which would 'upgrade' them to language status in due course. Books and articles are already appearing which (in their nomenclature, at least) anticipate such outcomes.[18] After all, if a community wished its way of speaking to be considered a 'language', and if they had the political power to support their decision, who would be able to stop them doing so? The present-day ethos is to allow communities to deal with their own internal policies themselves, as long as these are not perceived as being a threat to others. The scenario for the future of English is so complex and unpredictable, with many pidgins, creoles, and mixed varieties emerging and gradually acquiring prestige, that it is perfectly possible that in a few generations time the degree of local distinctiveness in a speech system, and the extent of its mutual unintelligibility with other historically related systems, will have developed to the extent that it will be given a name other than 'English'

---

[18] McArthur (1998), Rosen (1994), and the journal *World Englishes*. See also Crystal (1998).

(as has happened already – though not yet with much success – in the case of Ebonics). At such a time, a real evolutionary increase in the number of 'English languages' would have taken place. A similar development could affect any language that has an international presence, and where situations of contact with other languages are fostering increased structural diversity. The number of new pidgins and creoles is likely to be relatively small, compared with the rate of language loss, but they must not be discounted, as they provide evidence of fresh linguistic life.

Estimates about the number of languages in the world, therefore, must be treated with caution. There is unlikely to be any single, universally agreed total. As a result, it is always problematic translating observations about percentages of endangered languages into absolute figures, or vice versa. If you believe that 'half the languages in the world are dying', and you take one of the middle-of-the-road totals above, your estimate will be some 3,000 languages. But if you then take this figure out of the air (as I have seen some newspaper reporters do), and relate it to one of the higher estimates (such as the Global Language Register's 10,000), you would conclude that less than a third of the world's languages are dying – and, as a consequence, that the situation is not as serious as has been suggested. The fact that this reasoning is illegitimate – the criteria underlying the first total being very different from those underlying the second – is disregarded. And, as I read the popular press, I see all kinds of claims and counter-claims being made, with the statistics used to hold a weight of argument they cannot bear.

At the same time, despite the difficulties, we cannot ignore the need for global measures. As so much of the situation to be described below is bound up with matters of national and international policy and planning, we have to arrive at the best estimates we can, in order to persuade governments and funding bodies about the urgency of the need. Accordingly, I will opt for the range of 5,000–7,000 as my lower and upper bounds, for the year 2000 – 6±1K – and will relate any further talk of percentages to this.[19]

The size of the problem

A language is said to be dead when no one speaks it any more. It may continue to have existence in a recorded form, of course – traditionally in writing, more recently as part of a sound or video archive (and it does in a sense 'live

---

[19] As an endnote to this section, it is worth remembering that the languages we have today are only a fraction of all the languages there have ever been. There are too many unknowns for estimates to be other than highly speculative, but we can make some guesses using two criteria. First, we have some evidence from the known span of recorded Western history about the number of languages (and civilizations) that have died; and from historical linguistics we know something about the rate at which languages change – for example, the rise of the Romance languages from Vulgar Latin. We also have a vague idea about the age of the language faculty in humans, which probably arose between 100,000 and 20,000 years ago. Combining these variables is a daring task, but some people have attempted it. Pagel (1995: 6) concludes that there may have been as many as 600,000 languages spoken on earth, or as few as 31,000; his 'middle of the road' estimate is 140,000. Even if we take his lowest estimate, it is plain that far more languages have died, in the history of humankind, than now remain. For the question of whether the rate of decline has increased in recent times, see below; for the issue of what we may have lost, see chapter 2.

on' in this way) – but unless it has fluent speakers one would not talk of it as a 'living language'. And as speakers cannot demonstrate their fluency if they have no one to talk to, a language is effectively dead when there is only one speaker left, with no member of the younger generation interested in learning it. But what do we say if there are two speakers left, or 20, or 200? How many speakers guarantee life for a language?

It is surprisingly difficult to answer this question. One thing is plain: an absolute population total makes no sense. The analysis of individual cultural situations has shown that population figures without context are useless. In some circumstances, such as an isolated rural setting, 500 speakers could permit a reasonably optimistic prediction; in others, such as a minority community scattered about the fringes of a rapidly growing city, the chances of 500 people keeping their ethnic language alive are minimal. In many Pacific island territories, a community of 500 would be considered quite large and stable; in most parts of Europe, 500 would be minuscule. Speaker figures should never be seen in isolation, but always viewed in relation to the community to which they relate. Thus, in one survey, by Akira Yamamoto,[20] languages which had between 300 and 500 speakers included the Santa Ana dialect of Keresan (USA), Ulwa (Nicaragua), and Sahaptin (USA); but the first of these localities had a community population of only 600, the second had about 2,000, and the third had about 12,000. Plainly, the figure 500 tells a different story in each case, when it comes to evaluating the level of endangerment. Yamamoto concludes his survey with the comment that

[20] Yamamoto (1997: 12).

population size alone is not an accurate indicator of a language situation. He gives an example of a language which at the time of the survey had just 185 speakers of all ages – Karitiana (Brazil). Though this seems small, he points out that the total size of the community was only 191 – in other words, we have to say that over 96% of the people speak the language. And as the children are apparently continuing to learn Karitiana as their first language (with Portuguese coming later, as a second language), Yamamoto asks pertinently, is this really an endangered language?

The presumption is that any language which has a very small number of speakers is bound to be in trouble, and common sense tells us that this should usually be the case.[21] Perhaps only in places where the circumstances are especially favourable could such a language survive (see, further, chapter 3). So, notwithstanding the exceptions, most people would accept that a language spoken by less than 100 is in a very dangerous situation. They would then probably think in terms of a 'sliding scale' whereby languages with less than 500 would be somewhat less endangered, those with 1,000 even less so, and so on. What is unclear is the level at which we would stop automatically thinking in terms of danger. The figures suggested for this level are higher than we might expect.

---

[21] Many articles on endangered languages reflect this point: for example, Norris (1998: 3) says: 'There are a number of factors which contribute to a language's ability to survive. First and foremost is the size of the population with an Aboriginal mother tongue or home language. Since a large base of speakers is essential to ensure long-term viability, the more speakers a language has, the better its chances of survival.' See, further, chapter 4.

A total of 10,000 suggests safety in the short term, but not in the medium term.[22] In the savannah zone in Africa, for example, some linguists consider a language to be endangered if it has less than 20,000 speakers.[23] And in parts of West Africa, where English and French creoles in particular are attracting huge numbers of new speakers, many local languages are felt to be endangered – even though they are currently spoken by several hundred thousand. This is what surprises people – that languages with such large numbers of speakers can nonetheless be in danger. Yet, within the twentieth century, we have seen many languages fall from very large numbers: for example, in 1905 one estimate of Breton gave 1.4 million speakers; today, depending on the kind of fluency criteria used, the figure may be as low as 250,000.[24] And when we consider the causes of language death (chapter 3), it is evident that the factors involved are so massive in their effect that even a language with millions of speakers may not be safe. Even Yoruba, with 20 million speakers, has been called 'deprived' because of the way it has come to be dominated by English in higher education.[25] And during a visit to Southern Africa in 1998, speakers of several of the newly recognized official languages of South Africa expressed to me their anxiety for their long-term future, in the face of English – including several Afrikaners (whose language, Afrikaans, is spoken by around 6 million). The same reaction was observed in Zimbabwe, where not only

---

[22] For example, Dixon (1991: 231).
[23] Footnote to a field report on Kagoro (Mali) by Vydrine (1998: 3).
[24] Total given for 1991 in the Breton entry in Price (1998: 38).
[25] Brenzinger (1998: 93).

speakers of Ndebele (1.1 million) but even of Shona (7 million) professed the same anxiety. One experience illustrates the trend that these people find so worrying: engaging a Johannesburg driver in conversation, it transpired that he was conversant with all 11 of his country's official languages – an ability which he did not think at all unusual. However, his main ambition was to earn enough to enable all his children to learn English. None of the other languages ranked highly in his esteem.

Although concerns have been expressed about some languages with relatively large populations, it is the ones with the smallest totals which have inevitably captured the most attention. Yamamoto also recognizes this (see fn. 20 above): 'the number of speakers is an immediate index for its endangered situation'. It is difficult to see how a community can maintain its identity when its population falls beneath a certain level. Hence there is some force behind the statistics of language use which scholars have been compiling in recent years – though these surveys have not been taking place long enough for one to see long-term trends (e.g. whether there is an increase in the rate at which languages are being lost). An updated table in *Ethnologue* (February 1999) recognizes 6,784 languages, with data available for 6,059. Using this latter figure – and inevitably disregarding the question-marks which accompany several of the estimates – we can obtain the totals in Table 1, all for first language speakers.

There are many observations which can be made from a scrutiny of a summary table of this kind, and of the fuller table which underlies it. Beginning with the largest totals: it is evident that a very small number of languages accounts for a vast proportion of the world's population

Table 1

	N	%	Cumulative downwards%	Cumulative upwards%
more than 100 million	8	0.13		99.9
10–99.9 million	72	1.2	1.3	99.8
1–9.9 million	239	3.9	5.2	98.6
100,000–999,999	795	13.1	18.3	94.7
10,000–99,999	1,605	26.5	44.8	81.6
1,000–9,999	1,782	29.4	74.2	55.1
100–999	1,075	17.7	91.9	25.7
10–99	302	5.0	96.9	8.0
1–9	181	3.0	99.9	

(thought to have passed 6 billion in mid 1999). The 8 languages over 100 million (Mandarin, Spanish, English, Bengali, Hindi, Portuguese, Russian, Japanese) have nearly 2.4 billion speakers between them; and if we extend this count to include just the top 20 languages, we find a total of 3.2 billion – over half the world's population. If we continued the analysis downwards, we would eventually find that just 4% of the world's languages are spoken by 96% of the population.

Turning this statistic on its head: 96% of the world's languages are spoken by just 4% of the population. That is the perspective within which any discussion of language death must be seen. And, at the bottom end of the table, there are some sobering deductions. From the rightmost column, we can see that a quarter of the world's languages are spoken by less than 1,000 people; and well over half by less than 10,000. The median number of speakers for all languages in the list is 6,000. If the figure of 20,000 (referred to above as a danger-level in some parts of the world) were taken as a universal datum, this would correspond to exactly two-thirds of the world's languages. Then, using the leftmost column, we can see that nearly 500 languages have less than 100 speakers; around 1,500 have less than 1,000; and 3,340 have less than 10,000. If a population of 20,000 is again taken as a danger-level datum, we are talking about 4,000 languages. Most of these will be found in those parts of the world where languages are most numerous – notably in the equatorial regions everywhere (see fn. 12 above). The underlying table also lists 51 languages with just a single speaker – 28 in Australia, 8 in the USA, 3 in South America, 3 in Africa, 6 in Asia, 3 in the Pacific islands.

As we have already seen, conditions vary so much around the world that it is impossible to generalize from population alone about the rate at which languages die out. That is why there is so much variation in the claims that are currently being made, that 'x% of the world's languages are going to die out in the next 100 years' – x here has been anything from 25% (a conservative estimate which correlates with the 'less than 100' criterion) to 80% or more (a radical estimate which correlates with the 'less than 100,000' criterion). It is impossible, in our present state of knowledge, to say more about these deductions other than that they are well-informed guesswork. Most available demographic data (on death-rate, fertility-rate, etc.) is country-based, and not language-related. On the other hand, there have been enough micro-studies of specific locations carried out over a period of time to indicate the rate at which a downward trend operates. One report, on Dyirbal (Australia), found some 100 speakers in 1963, with everyone over about 35 speaking it as a first language; by 1993, there were just 6 speakers, all over about 65, with comprehension by some younger people.[26] Another report showed that in 1990 there were 60 fluent speakers of Aleut in Atka (USA), the main village where it survives; but by 1994 this number was down to 44, with the youngest speakers in their twenties.[27] At that rate of attrition, the language could stop being used by 2010.[28] (The factors which can influence the rate of decline are reviewed in chapter 3.)

Here is a more detailed example of the nature of a downwards trend. A Canadian census-based study[29] showed that between 1981 and 1996 most of Canada's 50 Aboriginal languages suffered a steady erosion; indeed, by the latter date only 3 of the languages were felt to have large enough populations to be secure from the threat of long-term extinction (Inuktitut, Cree, Ojibway).

[26] Dixon (1997: 105).

[27] Bergsland (1998: 38). Another example of a language which has gone from vital to moribund within a generation is Cup'ik in Chevak, Alaska: see Woodbury (1998: 239). The suddenness of the change in the languages of the Great Plains is emphasized in Furbee, Stanley, and Arkeketa (1998: 75).

[28] Another example of extrapolation is given for Tlingit and Haida in Dauenhauer and Dauenhauer (1998: 72): on the basis of current trends, if the youngest speaker of Tlingit is 45, and lives to be 100, the language will be dead in 2050. It should be noted that a pattern of decline is not always a smooth descending curve. There is evidence of a cyclical process in some places, as a period of loss is followed by one of maintenance. In parts of India, for example, there is evidence of people letting their indigenous language fall into disuse in early childhood, or after moving to a city to find work; but if they join new social networks after marriage, or return to their village with a newfound political awareness, they may then become actively involved in its resuscitation (Annamalai 1998: 25).

[29] Norris (1998).

A superficial look at the census data might suggest the contrary, for in this 15-year period the number of people reporting an indigenous mother tongue actually increased by 24% (chiefly the result of high fertility rates among the population). However, a closer look at the statistics shows a very different picture. There are four critical points (to each of which I add a general observation).

- The number of people who spoke an indigenous language at home grew by only 6%. In real terms, for every 100 people with an indigenous mother tongue, the number whose home language was most often an indigenous language declined from 76 to 65. (The importance of using the language at home is critical, in parts of the world where a population lives in relative isolation, and where it is unlikely that numbers will be enhanced through immigration. In the present survey, the viability of a language is directly reflected in its proportion of home language use: in the more viable languages, an average of 70 out of every 100 used their indigenous language at home; in the less viable ones, this had fallen to 30 or fewer.)[30]
- The age trend shows a steady decline: 60% of those aged 85+ used an indigenous mother tongue, compared

[30] Some demographers use an *index of continuity*, derived by dividing the number of people who speak an indigenous language at home by the number of those who speak it as a mother tongue. A figure of less than 100 indicates a decline in the viability of the language. Another measure is an *index of ability*, derived by dividing the number of mother-tongue users by the number of people who have reasonable conversational ability in it. A figure of more than 100 indicates the presence of second-language speakers, and thus the possibility of revival. See Harrison (1997).

with 30% of those aged 40–44, and 20% of children under 5. The average age of speakers of all indigenous languages rose from 28 to 31. (Age is another critical factor, as it shows the extent to which language transmission between generations has been successful. The lower the average language population age, the more successful the parents have been in getting young people to speak it. A rise in average speaker age is a strong predictor of a language's progress towards extinction.)

• The points at which language loss chiefly take place can also be identified: in 1981, 91 out of 100 children under 5 spoke their mother tongue at home; in 1996, these children had reached their late teens, and only 76 out of 100 now did so. (The ages at which there is a shift in language use are highly significant.[31] The dependence of very young children on their family means that few have an opportunity to shift from their home language. By contrast, the teenage years, characterized by pressure both from peer-group trends and from the demands of the job-market, are a particularly sensitive index of where a language is going.)

• The preceding point takes on fresh significance when people leave the family home. The data show that language loss is most pronounced during the early years

---

[31] *Language shift* is the conventional term for the gradual or sudden move from the use of one language to another (either by an individual or by a group). Other terms frequently encountered in the endangered languages literature include: *language loss*, for a situation where a person or group is no longer able to use a language previously spoken; *language maintenance*, where people continue to use a language, often through adopting specific measures; and *language loyalty*, which expresses the concern to preserve a language when a threat is perceived.

of entering the job-market and after marriage (especially among women): between ages 20 and 24, 74 out
of 100 women were using an indigenous language; but
in the corresponding group 15 years later, this average
had fallen to 45. (Such a shift is particularly serious, as
these are the years in which women are likely to be
bringing up their children. Fewer children are thus
going to be exposed to the indigenous language at
home.)

There are also several positive signs in the Canadian
situation; but the picture of overall decline is very clear,
and has its parallels in other census studies, notably in the
USA. These studies, however, provide only a very partial
picture of the world situation: most countries do not
record census data on language use at all, or (when they
do) the questions they ask do not throw light on the issue
of language endangerment.

It is certainly possible, after immersing yourself in data
of this kind, to 'take a view' (as lawyers say) about the
global situation, and several writers have done so. One of
the most widely quoted statistics is that of Michael
Krauss, who concludes, after a statistical review:[32]

I consider it a plausible calculation that – at the rate things are
going – the coming century will see either the death or the
doom of 90% of mankind's languages.

That means only about 600 are 'safe'. As I have already
indicated in my Preface, the groups which have been
established to monitor the situation are in total agreement
about the seriousness of the situation, though usually

---

[32] Krauss (1992: 7).

avoiding a hard statistic. For example, here are two judgements from the Foundation for Endangered Languages:[33]

The majority of the world's languages are vulnerable not just to decline but to extinction.

Over half the world's languages are moribund, i.e. not effectively being passed on to the next generation [see further below].

A middle position would assert 50% loss in the next 100 years. This is the view independently arrived at by three linguists reported by Krauss in 1992.[34] 50% is 3,000 languages. 100 years is 1,200 months. To meet that time frame, at least one language must die, on average, every two weeks or so. This cannot be very far from the truth.

Levels of danger

Comparing levels of endangerment is very difficult, in view of the diversity of language situations around the world, and the lack of theoretical models which would allow us to interpret combinations of relevant variables. How should we approach the kind of question raised earlier: which is the more endangered – a language where 400 people out of a community of 500 speak it, or one which has 800 speakers out of 1,000? Plainly, in such cases, the only answer is 'It all depends' – on such factors as the rate of acquisition by the children, the attitude of the whole community to it, and the level of impact of

---

[33] The first is from the preamble to the proposal to establish the Foundation for Endangered Languages, June 1995; the second is from *Iatiku* 2. 3.
[34] Krauss (1992: 6).

other languages which may be threatening it. At the same time, it is important for people to be able to take such factors into account (intuitively, at least, if surveys have not been made) and arrive at a judgement about just how endangered a language is. Some sort of classification of endangerment needs to be made. Without it, it would be impossible to 'take a view' about the urgency of the need, and thus to allocate scarce resources, in cases where something might be done (chapter 5).

A common-sense classification recognizes three levels: languages are **safe**, **endangered**, or **extinct**. To this, Michael Krauss adds a notion which has been widely taken up: languages which are no longer being learned as a mother tongue by children are said to be **moribund** (a term originating in the field of medicine).[35] This captures the notion of a language well beyond the stage of 'mere' endangerment, because it lacks intergenerational transmission; the analogy is with a .species unable to reproduce itself. The distinction is illustrated by Krauss with reference to North America, where he identifies a total of 187 indigenous languages. All are, in principle (given the dominant English-language environment), endangered; but major efforts are taking place in some communities to reverse the decline (see chapter 5). The more important statistic is to identify those which are moribund – which Krauss calculates to be 149, or 80%. In Alaska, the percentage is higher: there, only 2 out of the 20 indigenous languages were, in 1992, still being learned by children. A similar percentage is found in Australia. On the other hand, applying his criterion in South America

---

[35] Krauss (1992: 4).

produces a lower figure (27%) and in Central America an even lower one (17%).

Some classifications go a stage further, distinguishing 'safe' and 'not so safe', as in this five-level system:[36]

viable languages: have population bases that are sufficiently large and thriving to mean that no threat to long-term survival is likely;

viable but small languages: have more than *c.* 1,000 speakers, and are spoken in communities that are isolated or with a strong internal organization, and aware of the way their language is a marker of identity;

endangered languages: are spoken by enough people to make survival a possibility, but only in favourable circumstances and with a growth in community support;

nearly extinct languages: are thought to be beyond the possibility of survival, usually because they are spoken by just a few elderly people;

extinct languages: are those where the last fluent speaker has died, and there is no sign of any revival.

And here is a five-level classification used by Stephen Wurm, focusing on the weaker languages (and giving *moribund* a somewhat different emphasis):[37]

potentially endangered languages: are socially and economically disadvantaged, under heavy pressure

---

[36] Kincade (1991: 160–3).
[37] Wurm (1998: 192). Five-level models of status are typical: another is Bauman (1980), *who recognizes flourishing, enduring, declining, obsolescent, and extinct.*

from a larger language, and beginning to lose child speakers;

endangered languages: have few or no children learning the language, and the youngest good speakers are young adults;

seriously endangered languages: have the youngest good speakers age 50 or older;

moribund languages: have only a handful of good speakers left, mostly very old;

extinct languages: have no speakers left.

Another way of trying to introduce some order into endangerment is through the use of linguistic criteria, reflecting the range of functions for which languages are used and the types of structural change which they display. Endangered languages come to be used progressively less and less throughout the community, with some of the functions they originally performed either dying out or gradually being supplanted by other languages. There are many cases in Africa, for example, where an indigenous language has come to be less used in educational, political, and other public situations, because its roles have been taken over by English, Swahili, or some other lingua franca. In one formulation, such languages have been called 'deprived'.[38] Some languages suffer discourse attrition so much that they end up surviving in just one domain – for example, Ge'ez (Ethiopia) as a language of liturgy. Even modern European languages can feel the threat, as the following comment illustrates. Johan Van Hoorde is senior project manager at the Nederlandse

---

[38] Bamgbose (1997: 22).

Taalunie, an organization set up by the Dutch and Belgian governments to promote Dutch (currently spoken by *c.* 21 million):[39]

Dutch may not be threatened with extinction in the short or medium term, but it is in danger of losing domains. It could eventually become just a colloquial language, a language you use at home to speak with your family – the language you can best express your emotions in – but not the one you use for the serious things in life: work, money, science, technology.

From a structural point of view, different aspects of the language may show rapid change, amongst those people most influenced by it. There is usually a dramatic increase in the amount of codeswitching, with the threatened language incorporating features from the contact language(s). Grammatical features may be affected, such as an increase in the use of inflections and function words from the dominant language. Knowledge of vocabulary declines, with younger people familiar with only a proportion of the traditional vocabulary known by older people, and older people being unfamiliar with or antipathetic to the borrowed vocabulary that is replacing it. One study of Welsh looked at lexical erosion across three generations: three groups (N=20) of 60–80-year-olds, 40–59-year-olds, and 20–39-year-olds.[40] Everyone was asked to provide the Welsh word for 150 items belonging to domestic (weather, animals, parts of the body, clothing, etc.) and agricultural vocabulary. There was a steady decline in awareness between the generations: 65% of the senior group knew over 90% of the vocabulary, compared with

---

[39] Van Hoorde (1998: 6).   [40] Jones (1985).

40% of the middle-aged group – and none of the youngest group achieved the 90% level. The drop in the percentage of known items was greater in some semantic fields than others, being most noticeable in the vocabulary relating to parts of the body. In some languages, only one area of vocabulary may be left: an example is Yaku (Ethiopia), which is reported to survive in its plant names only.[41]

Assessing the level of functional or structural change in a language is an important process; but it must always be carried out with caution. After all, change is a normal and necessary part of all languages. Healthy languages are always borrowing from each other, and vocabulary is always changing between old and young generations. The formal characterization of what has been called language *obsolescence* is still in its early stages, as a research field, but its importance is evident. We need to know which features of change (if any) might be unambiguously associated with it.[42] When is the emergence or loss of a form, or the advent of a greater degree of language mixing, an instance of a 'change' introduced through the normal processes of language contact, and when is it an

---

[41] Report by Matthias Brenzinger to a seminar held at Dartmouth College, Hanover (New Hampshire, USA) in 1995 (reported in *Newsletter FEL* 1, p.5).

[42] The point is recognized by commentators in Dorian (1989): see especially the paper by Hoenigswald. The situation is not clear-cut. Romaine (1989) finds no factors functioning as exclusive predictors of language death. Also, considerable creativity is still possible, even in languages close to death. Endangered languages need to attract the same kind of theoretical investigation that has characterized the study of child language acquisition and pathological linguistic decline in individuals; see also Menn (1989).

instance of 'decline'? Normally, linguists fall over backwards to counter the purist view that linguistic change is
deterioration; and this stance needs to be used with
endangered languages too. But the kinds of change which
take place during the decline of endangered languages are
likely to be different from those which characterize
healthy languages. There are likely to be differences in
extent, range, rate, and quality: in a declining language,
far more features should be affected simultaneously; they
should belong to more areas of the language (e.g. different
aspects of grammar, different lexical fields); they should
change more rapidly; and they should change in the same
direction (displaying the influence of the languages which
are replacing them). Sometimes, the speed of change can
be dramatic indeed, resulting in a rapid and abrupt shift
with very little linguistic interference – what has been
called 'catastrophic' or 'radical' shift – a phenomenon
which has been noted, for example, in some African
situations where ethnicity is particularly weak while the
external pressure to shift is high.[43]

Conclusion

We frequently encounter dramatic and emotional reactions, when the topic turns to language death – and that is
hardly surprising, in view of the nature of the issues, and
the cultural realities which have led to so many languages
dying (see chapter 3). There are now several parts of the

---

[43] Examples are given in Tosco (1997). See also this assessment for
Quechua in Grinevald (1998: 139). The term *radical language shift* is
from Woodbury (1998: 235). Other terms have also been used, such as
language tip, in Dorian (1981: 51).

world where there are no indigenous languages left – for example, all the Arawakan and Cariban languages originally spoken in the islands of the Caribbean are now extinct. The drama has doubtless been unconsciously heightened by its coincidence with the millennium; but it is difficult to disagree with those who see the present time as a particularly critical moment in linguistic history:[44]

We, then, and our children, appear to live at the catastrophic inflexion point, where all together, for most languages in the world, the decline in speaker numbers reaches the zero point.

To support the use of such apocalyptic language, we need to let other voices be heard – insofar as this is possible, for those who are experiencing or have experienced language loss find it difficult to express their emotional state. What is it like to be without your rightful mother tongue? Hendrik Stuurman, talking about his Khoikhoi background in north-western South Africa, puts it this way:[45]

I feel that I have drunk the milk of a strange woman, that I grew up alongside another person. I feel like this because I do not speak my mother's language.

George Rizkalla, an Aramaic speaker from Malula, Syria, talks about the way in which Aramaic (currently spoken by c. 6,000 in three villages near Damascus) is gradually being displaced by Arabic:[46]

---

[44] Preamble to the proposal to establish a Foundation for Endangered Languages in the UK (Nicholas Ostler, June 1995). See also the quotations in my Preface.
[45] Report in the Braamfontein *Mail & Guardian* (Koch and Maslamoney 1997: 28).
[46] Report in the *Los Angeles Times* (Daniszewski 1997: A1).

Fifty years ago, all the students in Malula spoke Aramaic, and some of them could speak Arabic with difficulty. Now all speak Arabic, and some struggle with the Aramaic ... [*Then, talking about his children, who work in Damascus*] There they cannot see goats, or trees or peasants working in the field. So all the words for these things are forgotten because they hear such words maybe once a year. In this way the language gets poorer and poorer.

How can we sum up such an enormous concept as language death? Mari Rhydwen provides a relevant perspective:[47]

Loss of language is not the loss of a concept, an abstraction, but rather it is what happens when people change their behaviour and stop transmitting their language intergenerationally. It is intimately connected with people and it cannot be treated simply as an intellectual puzzle to be solved.

That is why so much of the contemporary emphasis, as we shall see in later chapters, is ecological in character, focusing on the relationships between people, their environment, and their thoughts and feelings.

For a modern literary comment, I call Scottish author James Kelman and Australian author David Malouf:[48]

My culture and my language have the right to exist, and no one has the authority to dismiss that.

When I think of my tongue being no longer alive in the mouths of men a chill goes over me that is deeper than my own death, since it is the gathered deaths of all my kind.

---

[47] Rhydwen (1998).
[48] Kalman, in a speech at the Booker Prize ceremony, 11 October 1994; Malouf (1985).

And for a classical literary comment, I call Samuel Johnson:[49]

My zeal for languages may seem, perhaps, rather overheated, even to those by whom I desire to be well esteemed. To those who have nothing in their thoughts but trade or policy, present power or present money, I should not think it necessary to defend my opinions; but with men of letters I would not unwillingly compound, by wishing the continuance of every language, however narrow in its extent, or however incommodious for common purposes, till it is reposited in some version of a known book, that it may be always hereafter examined and compared with other languages.

But why should these people, from the humble to the famous, think like this? Why is the issue of language death so important to them? Why should it be important to us? Why, in a phrase, should we care?[50]

---

[49] Samuel Johnson, 13 August 1766, letter to William Drummond, in Boswell (1791: ch. 18).

[50] Two important books, which appeared at virtually the same time as the first edition of *Language Death*, are Nettle and Romaine (2001) and Hagège (2001), the former containing much more of an anthropological frame of reference, the latter much more of a philosophical perspective. Their near-simultaneous appearance testifies to the growing sense of urgency among professionals about the matter, and their mutually reinforcing message has significantly increased public awareness and debate about the issue.

2

Why should we care?

~

Many people think we shouldn't. There is a widely held
and popular – but nonetheless misconceived – belief that
any reduction in the number of languages is a benefit for
mankind, and not a tragedy at all. Several strands of
thought feed this belief. One reflects the ancient tradition,
expressed in several mythologies but most famously in the
Biblical story of Babel, that the proliferation of languages
in the world was a penalty imposed on humanity, the
reversal of which would restore some of its original
perfectibility.[1] In an ideal world, according to this view,
there would be just one language, which would guarantee
mutual understanding, enlightenment, and peace. Any
circumstances which reduce the number of languages in
the world, thereby enabling us to move closer to this goal,
must therefore be welcomed.

There are two intractable difficulties with this view.
The first is the naivety of the conception that sharing a
single language is a guarantor of mutual understanding
and peace, a world of new alliances and global solidarity.
The examples to the contrary are so numerous that it
would be impracticable to list them. Suffice it to say that
all the major monolingual countries of the world have had
their civil wars, and that as one reflects on the war-zones
of the world in the last decades of the twentieth century, it

[1] See Eco (1995); for the comparative dimension, see Borst (1957–63).

is striking just how many of them are in countries which are predominantly monolingual – Vietnam, Cambodia, Rwanda, and Burundi (the latter two standing out in Africa in their lack of multilingualism). It is, in short, a total myth that the sharing of a single language brings peace, whichever language it might be. It is difficult to see how the eventual arrival of English, Esperanto, or any other language as a global lingua franca could eliminate the pride that leads to ambition and conflict – any more than it did in the supposed unilingual pre-Babelian era.[2]

The second difficulty, of course, relates to this question of choice. The people who are most vociferously in favour of a single world language tend to come from major monolingual nations, and make the assumption that, when the day arrives, it will be their own language which, of course, everyone will use. Problems arise when, for religious, nationalistic, or other reasons, the vote goes in different directions, as it has always done. The oldest debate has as its focus the nature of the imagined first language of mankind – a debate which has generated

---

[2] 'Supposed', because Genesis 10 lists the sons of Japheth 'according to their countries and each of their languages', and Babel did not take place until later. Eco (1995: 10) notices this point, referring to it as 'a chink in the armour of the myth of Babel', and comments: 'If languages were differentiated not as a punishment but simply as a result of a natural process, why must the confusion of tongues constitute a curse at all?' Note also the belief that Iatiku, goddess of the Acoma tribe of New Mexico, is said to have caused people to speak different languages so that they would find it less easy to quarrel. The underlying truth here is the source of ironic comment in *The hitch-hiker's guide to the galaxy* (Adams, 1979: ch. 6), which reports that the instantaneous translator of the future, called the Babel fish, 'by effectively removing all barriers to communication between different races and cultures, has caused more and bloodier wars than anything else in the history of creation'.

centuries of pointless but hotly partisan speculation. According to Dante, in *De vulgari eloquentia*, 'Hebrew was the language which the lips of the first speaker formed.'[3] Dante could claim a great deal of support, but there have been many who would disagree – such as the lady at the Versailles court who said (according to Voltaire): 'What a great shame that the bother at the tower of Babel should have got language all mixed up; but for that, everyone would always have spoken French.'[4] German, Egyptian, and Chinese have all had their supporters, as have many other languages.[5] More recently, looking forwards rather than backwards, there are those who expect a future single world language to come through the intervention of an international organization of some kind – though when we see the many conflicts around the world which arise when people believe their language is being sidelined (Quebec, Belgium, and India provide instances which regularly reach the headlines), it is virtually impossible to conceive of a situation in which an international body could persuade people to voluntarily give up their language, or support another at the expense of their own. The reasons for this I shall discuss below.

None of this, it should be clear, has anything to do with the perceived value of a language becoming a global lingua franca. Lingua francas have an obvious and important role in facilitating international communication; but even if one language does, through some process of linguistic evolution, become the world's lingua franca – a

---

[3] Dante (*c.* 1304), part I, ch. 6.
[4] Voltaire, Letter to Catherine the Great, 26 May 1767.
[5] For other examples, see Crystal (1985: 48).

status which most people feel is likely to be held by English[6] – it does not follow that this must be at the expense of other languages. A world in which everyone speaks at least two languages – their own ethnic language and an international lingua franca – is perfectly possible, and (as I shall argue below) highly desirable. Because the two languages have different purposes – one for identity, the other for intelligibility – they do not have to be in conflict. However, persuading individual governments to work towards a bilingual (or multilingual) world is by no means easy, not least because of the costs involved; and the history of individual language situations, invariably containing elements of colonial exploitation, can be so full of emotion that conflict is at least as common as concord.

Emotions regularly cloud the issues. People who are prepared to grant that, on a global scale, language loss is a bad thing, can sometimes nonetheless be heard condemning a locally encountered language, along with the culture of which it is a part. Frequently, this is part of a history of ethnic conflict, or a cultural clash between classes, as when suburban dwellers encounter a population of Rom travellers. The fears may be real or imagined, and they will almost certainly be fed by a history of stereotyping; but the resulting condemnation is the same: *most* languages are fine, but *their* language is 'foul-mouthed', 'primitive', and 'little more than noise', and 'it wouldn't be a bad thing if it disappeared'. Facts come to be beside the point in such situations – notably the fact (which

---

[6] I review this case in Crystal (1997b); a more sceptical view of the long-term position of English is Graddol (1997).

I shall illustrate below) that there is no such thing as a primitive language, and that every language is capable of great beauty and power of expression.[7] Fears and hatreds pay no attention to facts.

Sometimes it is reason which clouds the issues – a reason, that is, which seems plausible when you first hear it, but which with further thought turns out to be spurious. The most commonly heard argument here is the economic one: having so many languages in the world is a waste of money, because individuals and firms have to spend so much time and energy on translating and interpreting. If there were just one language, so this argument goes, everyone could get on with the job of buying and selling without having to worry about these barriers. There is an element of truth in this: it does indeed cost a lot of money to cope with the diversity of the world's languages. The fallacy is to think that it is money wasted. Indeed, the view that foreign languages get in the way of buying and selling has been frequently countered, in recent years, by evidence from the business world itself, where knowledge of a foreign language is so often seen to be a competitive advantage. Given two British firms,

---

[7] For a classic statement on the misconceptions of primitiveness, see Hymes (1966: 74): 'we know no natural languages with vocabularies so limited that their speakers must eke them out with gestures (and hence perhaps cannot communicate in the dark); which lack definite systems of sounds and grammar; which lack standards of usage; which, because of lack of system or of writing, change more rapidly in structure than other languages; which lack abstract terms or capacity for forming them; which cannot serve significant intellectual and aesthetic expression. We know, indeed, no demonstrated characteristics which would place together the languages of "primitive" peoples as against those of "civilized" peoples.' For a recent affirmation, see Dixon (1997: 65, 118). See further below.

trying to sell to the Arabic market, and one is capable of using Arabic and the other is not – all else being equal, which firm do you think will more impress the buyer? Languages, it has been well said, are the lubricant of trade.[8]

There are strong economic arguments available to counter the 'many-languages-wasteful' view.[9] For example, from the viewpoint of 'human capital theory', language is part of the resources people can draw upon in order to increase the value of their potential contribution to productivity. A cost-benefit analysis of the consequences of being multilingual would bring to light a wide range of benefits for individuals, both financial and non-financial (e.g. in terms of achieving wider horizons or wider social acceptance). This would form part of a much broader economic perspective, in which the traditional view, that the economy influences language, is supplemented by the notion that language exercises a strong influence on the economy. There are several domains in which languages play an important role, and thus contribute to their economic success – such as tourism (with its emphasis on diversity), the arts, and local manufacturing industries. Local languages are seen to be valuable because they promote community cohesion and vitality, foster pride in a culture, and give a community (and thus a workforce)

---

[8] Arcand (1996: 119).

[9] Very little study has been devoted to what might be called the 'economics' or 'market value' of language; an exception is the 1996 issue of the *International Journal of the Sociology of Language* on 'Economic Approaches to Language and Language Planning'; see, especially in relation to the point about 'buying and selling', the paper by Grin. See also Coulmas (1992).

self-confidence. In just the same way as so much of language shift has been shown to result from economic factors, so these same factors can be used to foster language maintenance. People it seems are willing to devote large sums of money to having their identity promoted. It can, in short, pay you to be bilingual – where the 'you' can be an individual, a business, or a government. We shall return to the point below.

There is no plausibility in the view 'the fewer languages the better', to my mind; the opposite view, however, has several strong arguments. So, what are the benefits of maintaining as many of the world's languages as possible? The issues do need to be formally laid out, for it has to be admitted that problems to do with language – like many other domains which chiefly influence the quality of life (such as speech therapy, or the arts) – do not make as immediate an impression on human consciousness as do the consequences of, say, famine or disease. The loss of a language is not self-evidently life-threatening. Nor has the language issue attracted the public attention in the same way as has the issue of the environment.[10] Most adults know, and all children are taught, about such matters as the need to conserve the world's rainforests and its ecological diversity. The green movement has been

---

[10] The contrast in the public awareness of biological and of linguistic diversity has been noted by several commentators: see Hale (1992a: 1), Krauss (1992: 7), and Rhydwen (1998: 101–2). The hundreds of international and national organizations devoted to botanical and zoological endangerment, some of which have passed their century (e.g. the National Audubon Society, for the conservation of birds in the USA, was founded in 1866), contrasts strikingly with the tiny handful of linguistic organizations which began to appear in the mid-1990s. See further below.

eminently successful in raising the public consciousness and sense of urgency about its biological heritage – in all domains except language. There has been little public perception of the need for a 'green linguistics'.[11] The arguments have only recently been marshalled, and have received little publicity. It is high time for them to reach a wider public. There are basically five of them, all answering in different ways the question 'Why should we care if a language dies?'

Because we need diversity

This is a direct extension of the ecological frame of reference: the arguments which support the need for biological diversity also apply to language. Most people, in fact, would accept without need for argument the proposition that ecological diversity is a good thing, and that its preservation should be fostered. But if we look at the reasoning which underlies this view, we find two issues which need to be made explicit if the application of ecological thinking to language is to be clear. First, in relation to ecology: it is not simply that an individual species is of interest or value in its own right. The whole concept of the ecosystem is based on the insight that living entities exist through a network of interrelationships. To take just one definition: an ecosystem is 'the system formed by the interaction of all living organisms, plants, animals,

---

[11] Notwithstanding the unconscious advertising of the matter by Chomsky (1957: 15)! Within linguistics, the field of ecolinguistics has been steadily growing: see the review by Fill (1998), Fill and Mulhausler (2001), and p. 94 below.

bacteria, etc. with the physical and chemical factors of their environment'.[12] In a holistic conception, the cultural as well as the biological domains are brought into a mutually reinforcing relationship: the distinctive feature of human ecology is accordingly the attempt 'to link the structure and organization of a human community to interactions with its localized environment'.[13] And a major emphasis in this literature is that damage to any one of the elements in an ecosystem can result in unforeseen consequences for the system as a whole.

The second issue focuses on the notion of diversity, which also has considerable relevance. The world is 'incorrigibly plural' (as Louis MacNeice put it in 'Snow', 1935). Diversity has a central place in evolutionary thought, where it is seen as the result of species genetically adapting in order to survive in different environments: 'Evolution depends on genetic diversity.'[14] Increasing uniformity holds dangers for the long-term survival of a species. In the language of ecology: the strongest ecosystems are those which are most diverse. As one author has put it, 'The diversity of living things is apparently directly correlated with stability ... variety may be a necessity in

[12] Kenneth Mellanby, entry on 'ecosystem' in Bullock, Stallybrass, and Trombley (1988: 253).

[13] Peter Haggett, entry on 'human ecology' in Bullock, Stallybrass, and Trombley (1988: 248). The parallels between the way an 'ideology of death' is affecting both biosphere and culture are drawn in Babe (1997). See, further, chapter 4 below.

[14] Steve Jones, in Jones, Martin and Pilbeam (1992: 269). It should be noted that the genetic analogy can take us only so far: there is no case for a Darwinian perspective, in which we note dispassionately the survival of the linguistic fittest, because the factors which cause the death of languages are, in principle, very largely under human control.

the evolution of natural systems.'[15] And, in its application to human development, the point has often been made that our success in colonizing the planet has been due to our ability to develop diverse cultures which suit all kinds of environments.

The need to maintain linguistic diversity stands squarely on the shoulders of such arguments. If diversity is a prerequisite for successful humanity, then the preservation of linguistic diversity is essential, for language lies at the heart of what it means to be human. If the development of multiple cultures is so important, then the role of languages becomes critical, for cultures are chiefly transmitted through spoken and written languages. Accordingly, when language transmission breaks down, through language death, there is a serious loss of inherited knowledge: 'Any reduction of language diversity diminishes the adaptational strength of our species because it lowers the pool of knowledge from which we can draw.'[16] For the individual speakers, it is a significant loss, because their personal history has gone; but this loss has an indirect effect on everyone (as I shall illustrate below). One field linguist put it this way: 'A native language is like a natural resource which cannot be replaced once it is removed from the earth.'[17] Another commentator adopts a zoological parallel: 'just as the extinction of any animal species diminishes our world, so does the extinction of any language'.[18] A third adopts a genetic analogy: 'Language

---

[15] Odum (1986).   [16] Bernard (1992: 82).

[17] Romeo Labillos, in Maurais (1996: 269).

[18] Hale (1992a: 8). The principle expressed by Hale and other contributors to that issue of *Language* was attacked by Peter Ladefoged in a subsequent issue (Ladefoged 1992), challenging the assumption that

diversity, like a gene pool, is essential for our species to thrive ... If we are to prosper, we need the cross-fertilisation of thought that multilingualism gives us.'[19] And a policy statement issued by the Linguistic Society of America in 1994 goes a step beyond analogy:[20]

The loss to humankind of genetic diversity in the linguistic world is ... arguably greater than even the loss of genetic diversity in the biological world, given that the structure of human language represents a considerable testimony to human intellectual achievement.

A notion such as 'cross-fertilization of thought' sounds very simple; but it is far more than allowing oneself to be influenced by the occasional foreign turn of phrase – as when English speakers make use of such words as *elan* or *chic*. For bilingual (or multilingual) individuals, there is the permanent availability of two (or more) hugely different perspectives on large areas of life. And even monolingual people are historically multilingual, in the

different languages and cultures always ought to be preserved. His point was that, when political considerations are taken into account – as they always must be – linguists are not best placed to make a value judgement about whether a language should be preserved or not. There is an enormous distance between the axiom of desirable diversity and its application in individual circumstances. This point is discussed further in chapter 4.

[19] Pogson (1998: 4). An ecological perspective has been adopted by many linguists working with endangered languages: see, for example, Wurm (1991: 2–4), and below, chapter 4, fn. 6.

[20] Committee on Endangered Languages and their Preservation (1994: 5). Peter Trudgill (1991) makes the interesting point that languages as partial barriers to communication are actually a good thing, ecologically speaking, because they make it more difficult for dominant cultures to penetrate smaller ones; see also Trudgill (2000: ch. 9).

sense that their language will contain loan-words reflecting the history of its contact with other cultures. English, for example, has borrowed huge numbers of words from over several hundred languages, and hundreds of languages have in turn borrowed huge numbers of English words. That is what gives so much interest and variety to a lexicon, of course – in the case of English, an Anglo-Saxon word like *kingly* co-exists with a French word (*royal*) and a Latin word (*regal*), thereby offering possibilities of nuance and style which would not otherwise be available.

There is a second way in which a language contains our history. Through the words and idioms it uses, it provides us with clues about the earlier states of mind of its speakers, and about the kinds of cultural contact they had. There are over 350 living languages listed in the etymological files of the *Oxford English Dictionary*. Each etymology demonstrates through its presence a point of contact, an index of influence. Words become part of the evidence of social history. George Steiner's comment applies: 'Everything forgets. But not a language.'[21] With tens of thousands of words, idioms, and metaphors in a language's domestic vocabulary, and large numbers of grammatical constructions available to manipulate these items, it is plain that the potential for linguistic interaction, even between two languages, is immense. And with thousands of languages in the 'pool', the capabilities of expression stemming from the human language capacity are almost unimaginable. It is a richness of heritage whose power to facilitate individual expression, in the

---

[21] 'The hollow miracle', in Steiner (1967: 131).

form of community or personal identity, is virtually unlimited. Michael Krauss drives the point home:[22]

Surely, just as the extinction of any animal species diminishes our world, so does the extinction of any language. Surely we linguists know, and the general public can sense, that any language is a supreme achievement of a uniquely human collective genius, as divine and endless a mystery as a living organism. Should we mourn the loss of Eyak or Ubykh any less than the loss of the panda or California condor?

And Russian writer Vjaceslav Ivanov sums it up in this way:[23]

Each language constitutes a certain model of the universe, a semiotic system of understanding the world, and if we have 4,000 different ways to describe the world, this makes us rich. We should be concerned about preserving languages just as we are about ecology.

If there are 6,000 languages, of course (see p. 14), we are even richer. And if, in a century's time, as many have died as current fears predict, we will have lost half our traditional cultural wealth, and reduced our human expressive potential in proportion. (The possibility that some of this wealth might eventually be replaced is addressed in chapter 5.)

Because languages express identity

If we turn the concept of diversity over, we find identity. And everyone cares about their identity. A Welsh proverb

---

[22] Krauss (1992: 8).   [23] Ivanov (1992).

captures the essence of this section's answer to the question 'Why should we care if languages die?':

> Cenedl heb iaith, cenedl heb galon
> 'A nation without a language is a nation without a heart'

Even monolingual speakers of thriving languages can develop a sense of what it means to talk of endangered languages in terms of identity. All they have to do is reflect on the role of dialect within their community. I have never met anyone who, when presented with the issue, has failed to regret the passing of old rural dialects of British English, whether they are a member of a rural dialect community or not. Those who are concerned about the matter often form themselves into dialect societies, compiling lists of old words, preserving old stories, and sometimes engaging in translations of major works into dialect – extracts from Shakespeare or the Bible, for example.[24] Some of these bodies have been around a long time. The Yorkshire Dialect Society celebrated its centenary in 1997.

Few people have captured the romanticism and nostalgia that accompanies the dialect ethos better than Samuel Bamford, who made a collection of south Lancashire dialect words and phrases in 1854:[25]

> There is . . . a pleasure in the contemplation, the remembrance, as it were, through history, of old people who have left the place we live in, who have quitted the ground we occupy, who have just, as it were, gone out and shut the door of the house after them before we got in. We wish to recal [sic] them; we would

---

[24] As in Kellett (1996).   [25] Bamford (1854: xi–xii).

they had stayed a little longer; that they had been there when we arrived. We go to the door and look for them; up the street, down the lane, over the meadow, by the wood; but the old folks are not to be seen high or low, far or near; and we return to our room disappointed. We picture to ourselves the pleasant time we should have had were they beside us; how we should have seen the cut of their apparel, their broad hats, and quaint lappels [*sic*], their 'buckles and shoon'; and heard their old tales and stories, and caught the tones of their voice, and the accent of their uncouth words. But it cannot be; they are gone, and there is no return: we have not seen them, we never shall see them; and again we are saddened and disappointed. A book, however, in the midst of our regret, attracts our notice; we open it, and herein we find, not only the portraiture of those we have been regretting, but their old stories, their uncouth words, and almost the tones of their voice are therein preserved for us. We sit down happy in the prize, and enjoy the mental pleasure which it provides. Such a book would I place on the shelf of the old house ere I depart.

The sentimentality of the writing is typical of the genre, and doubtless there are those, accustomed to the harder tones of late twentieth-century discourse, who will find it unappealing. But the emotion it expresses should not be mocked, for it is genuine enough, and I quote it at length because it can help convey to those who are unused to the concept of language death something of the state of mind of those for whom that prospect is all too real. Such strength of feeling, one might reflect – and all for 'just' an endangered dialect! How much more emotion would one be justified in expressing, therefore, if we were dealing with an endangered language?

The word 'just' may be rhetorically appropriate, but it is of course cognitively a nonsense. For dialects are just as complex as languages in their sounds, grammar, vocabulary, and other features. As we have already seen in chapter 1, the boundary between dialect and language is arbitrary, dependent on sociopolitical considerations that can transform a dialect into a language at the drop of a bomb.[26] Dialect death *is* language death, albeit on a more localized scale. So the yearning for continuity which that quotation reflects will still be there, when it comes to considering the broader issues of language death. In both cases, we are dealing with issues of cultural distinctiveness, of a community's character, insofar as they are transmitted through language. These notions are intertwined. Character is the result of inheritance. As Thomas Mann remarked: 'We should know how to inherit, because inheriting is culture.'[27] But to know what it is that we inherit, we need language. Marianne Mithun, reflecting on work with North American peoples, sums it up in this way:[28]

The loss of languages is tragic precisely because they are not interchangeable, precisely because they represent the distillation of the thoughts and communication of a people over their entire history.

That is why, she goes on, an approach to these languages which tries to preserve them through translation only is misconceived:

[26] The military allusion is apt, for a language has been famously defined as 'a dialect with an army and a navy' (Weinreich, 1980). It is also apt for another reason: in so many instances the reasons for language loss, as we shall see in chapter 3, are bound up with military invasion. For a relevant dialectological study, see Holloway (1997).

[27] Quoted in Henze (1982).   [28] Mithun (1998: 189).

Language instruction and documentation that is limited to translations of English words or even English sentences misses the point entirely. It must capture not just how things are said, but also what people choose to say, not only in ceremonies and narrative, but in daily conversation as well.

Oliver Wendell Holmes captures the linguistic side to community character in a typically figurative expression: 'Every language is a temple, in which the soul of those who speak it is enshrined.'[29] It is a fine metaphor, though a somewhat passive one. It underplays the dynamic role which everyone has as active participants in their culture. We make culture, as well as receive it. A more appropriate analogy, accordingly, is to talk about cultural identity in terms of the self-expression of a people, however this is manifested. Rituals, music, painting, crafts, and other forms of behaviour all play their part; but language plays the largest part of all. Some would go much further: 'Language ... is not only an element of culture itself; it is the basis for all cultural activities.'[30] Although there are problems with 'all', as we shall see in chapter 4, those who work with endangered languages readily recognize the thrust of this point, for they see, day by day, the way a

---

[29] Holmes (1860: ch. 2).

[30] Bloch and Trager (1942: 5). We must be careful not to overstate this position. To anticipate the argument of chapter 4: the view that 'people cannot save their culture without their language' is one such overstatement, given that so many communities demonstrate a living ethnicity despite the fact that most of its members have lost or never learned the language. One of the most heated controversies in contemporary Wales, for example, is whether one can be Welsh if one does not speak Welsh; and there are arguments on both sides. The general issue needs research: which aspects of culture, exactly, are dependent on language for their preservation and which are not?

community is heavily dependent on language for communicating and interpreting its behaviour. 'What do you think?' 'What are they doing?' 'Why did she do that?' 'Who is that person?' These are not only the questions of outside analysts trying to make sense of their observations. They are questions which the members of a community ask of each other. Ultimately, to make sense of a community's identity, we need to look at its language.

Identity is what makes the members of a community recognizably the same. It is a summation of the characteristics which make it what it is and not something else – of 'us' vs 'them'. These characteristics may be to do with physical appearance, but just as often (especially in these increasingly heterogeneous days, when it can be difficult to tell what community people belong to just by looking at their faces) they relate to local customs (such as dress), beliefs, rituals, and the whole panoply of personal behaviours. And of all behaviours, language is the most ubiquitous. It is available even when we cannot see other people (shouting at a distance) or see anything at all (talking in the dark). Language is the primary index, or symbol, or register of identity. I search for the best metaphor, as have others before me. 'A language is the emblem of its speakers', says Dixon.[31] 'Language is a skin', says Barthes, 'I rub my language against another language.'[32] Emerson gives us a fine image:[33]

We infer the spirit of the nation in great measure from the language, which is a sort of monument to which each forcible individual in a course of many hundred years has contributed a stone.

[31] Dixon (1997: 135).   [32] Barthes (1977).
[33] In 'Nominalist and realist' (Emerson 1844).

In the case of the literary classics, the stones are massive indeed. And this historical slant is echoed by Edward Sapir:[34]

Language is the most massive and inclusive art we know, a mountainous and anonymous work of unconscious generations.

Identity, then, brings us inexorably into contact with history, which provides us with another way of answering the question 'Why should we care about language death?'

Because languages are repositories of history

On his tour of Scotland with James Boswell, Dr Johnson produced one of the remarks for which he is justly famous:[35]

Alas! sir, what can a nation that has not letters [=writing] tell of its original? I have always difficulty to be patient when I hear authors gravely quoted, as giving accounts of savage nations, which accounts they had from the savages themselves. What can the M'Craas tell about themselves a thousand years ago? There is no tracing the connection of ancient languages, but by language; and therefore I am always sorry when any language is lost, because languages are the pedigree of nations.

Some of his vocabulary is unpalatable nowadays, but his final observation is unassailable. Languages as the

---

[34] Sapir (1921: 220).
[35] In Boswell (1785): the day is 18 September 1773. 'M'Craas' is the name of one of the Scottish clans.

pedigree of nations. *Pedigree*, then as now, refers to ancestry, lineage, or descent. Johnson is thinking like a philologist, when he talks about a language's 'original'. But languages, once they are written down, tell us more than their philological connections. A language encapsulates its speakers' history. 'Language is the archives of history', said Emerson.[36] It does this, most obviously, by expressing, through the grammar and lexicon of its texts, the events which form its past.[37] Even the most casual glance at the reference section of any library conveys the extent to which people are reliant on written language for a full sense of their origins and development, as a nation. The literature section makes the point just as strongly. And, as individuals, we value highly those linguistic scraps of personal documentation which have come down to us from our ancestors – a grandparent's diary, the name scribbled on the back of a photograph, the entries in parish registers and gravestone inscriptions – all of which provide evidence of our own pedigree. We value the right to have this information ourselves; we take pride in it, and find in it a source of great pleasure and inspiration. Might we not, then, justifiably feel concerned to hear that others will not have access to this right? The desire to know about our ancestry is a universal inclination – but it takes a language to satisfy it. And, once a language is lost, the links with our past are gone. We are, in effect, alone.

[36] In 'The poet' (Emerson 1844).
[37] The links between word history and social history are well explored in Hughes (1988); see, for example, the history of culinary vocabulary on his p. 22.

Johan Van Hoorde seems to be making a similar point, in his comment: 'When you lose your language, . . . you exclude yourself from your past.'[38] But he is speaking as the project manager for Nederlandse Taalunie, and the context of his thinking is Dutch, a language which has been written down for centuries. The issue is therefore rather different. From Johnson we can sense the need to begin a period of linguistic continuity. From Van Hoorde, we can sense what happens when we end one: a new generation finds itself unable to reach into its history without special (philological) help. In this case, the texts are there, but inaccessible to the ordinary person. For mother-tongue English speakers, the nearest we can get to the 'feel' of this situation is with Old English: walk round a museum displaying Anglo-Saxon remains, and there is an artefactual continuity with the present-day which we can recognize; but encounter an Anglo-Saxon manuscript, and the language barrier is almost total. Anyone who feels that the language is denying them access to their legitimate history is right; but at 1,000 years' remove, the engaging of emotions tends to be more cerebral than heartfelt. By contrast, when we are unable to understand the letters of a dead grandfather or grandmother, because we no longer share a language with them, the poignancy can be inexpressible.

And if your language has never been written down? Johnson radically underestimates the abilities of oral performers. What can they tell about 1,000 years ago? A great deal, as we now know from studies of oral

---

[38] Van Hoorde (1998: 8).

traditions.[39] Mamadou Kouyate, a West African *griot* (oral performer) expresses it vividly:[40]

We are vessels of speech, we are the repositories which harbour secrets many centuries old ... We are the memory of mankind; by the spoken word we bring to life the deeds and exploits of kings for younger generations.

It is easy to think that such claims are flights of fancy; but they are not. Oral performers use sophisticated linguistic techniques to ensure the transmission of this memory. We ought not to be surprised. We are used to seeing prodigious feats of memory in, for example, concert soloists as they perform all of a composer's works without a sheet of music in front of them. Ask them how they do it, and they talk about developing wider perceptions of structural organization, operating with different kinds of memory simultaneously, and downgrading matters of detail – 'The memory is in the fingers', as concert pianist Iwan Llewellyn Jones put it to me once.[41] The oral performer also develops an overall sense of structure, intuiting a picture of the text as a whole, and leaving points of linguistic detail to 'look after themselves'. A professional story-teller 'knows' how points in a story coincide with crescendos and diminuendos, with allegros and lentos. It is a skill which can be observed even in very young children – for example, in the formulaic patterns

[39] See, for example, Lord (1960) on the oral songs of Yugoslav epic singers; Swann (1992), for a wide range of Amerindian illustrations; and, for a general review of the oral performance field, Edwards and Sienkewicz (1990).
[40] In Edwards and Sienkewicz (1990: 15).
[41] For cognitive musicology, see Sloboda (1986).

heard in 'knock knock' jokes, with their fixed sequences of intonation, rhythm, and loudness. In the professional, the sequences become elaborated indeed, incorporating a wide range of repetitive motifs, figures of speech, patterns of verbal elaboration (e.g. for praising, boasting, abusing), formulaic exaggerations, points of digression, and other linguistic devices, many of which act as the 'keys and scales' of oral performance. The analogy with music is not far-fetched, for much oral performance was in fact chanted or sung. And we know how extensive and sophisticated some of these performances could be, for we are fortunate to have some written versions preserved, such as the saga of Beowulf. The knowledge content can be enormous, including long lists of gods or kings, accounts of victories and defeats, stories of legends and heroes, details of recipes and remedies, and all the insights into past social structure and behaviour which we associate with any culture's mythology and folklore. Kouyate's claim to be a living memory therefore has to be taken very seriously indeed. And the thought that such living memories might be lost is therefore a matter of profound significance to those who need to rely on such performers to provide their only sense of ethnic origins.

Because languages contribute to the sum of human knowledge

Identity and history combine to ensure that each language reflects a unique encapsulation and interpretation of human existence, and this gives us yet another reason for caring when languages die. It is a motive that is more self-serving than altruistic, though no less worthy.

We should care – because we can learn a great deal from them.

The view that languages other than our own provide us with a means of personal growth, as human beings, is a recurrent theme in literature, at various levels of intellectual profundity. Several proverbial expressions have captured the essential insight.[42] From Slovakia: 'With each newly learned language you acquire a new soul.' From France: 'A man who knows two languages is worth two men.' Emerson takes up this theme:[43]

As many languages as he has, as many friends, as many arts and trades, so many times is he a man.

The message is clearly that there is much to be learned and enjoyed in experiencing other languages. And the corollary is that we miss out on this experience if we do not avail ourselves of the opportunity to encounter at least one other language. Everyone who has travelled has felt this limitation, to at least some extent. Here is Emerson again: 'No man should travel until he has learned the language of the country he visits. Otherwise he voluntarily makes himself a great baby, – so helpless and so ridiculous.'[44] There is a real sense in which a monolingual person, with a monolingual temperament, is disadvantaged, or deprived.

---

[42] See the collection in Champion (1938). There are corresponding insights in several of the countries covered by this book.

[43] 'Culture', in Emerson (1860).

[44] Emerson (1833/1909). It should by now be apparent that, to my mind, the writing of this author has a great deal to offer by way of insight into language. The essays from which these quotations are taken provide a great deal more.

Monolingual people need time to take in this point. And so, before resuming the argument, it is worth a paragraph of digression to stress that there are good grounds for conceiving the natural condition of the human being to be multilingual. The human brain has the natural capacity to learn several languages, and most members of the human race live in settings where they naturally and efficiently use their brains in precisely this way. Half the human race is known to be at least bilingual, and there are probably half as many bilinguals again in those parts of the world where there have been no studies, though cultural contacts are known to be high.[45] People who belong to a predominantly monolingual culture are not used to seeing the world in this way, because their mindset has been established through centuries of being part of a dominant culture, in which other people learn your language and you do not learn theirs. It is notable that the nations which are most monolingual in ability and attitude are those with a history of major colonial or religious expansion – their roles, in the West, reflected chiefly in the former or present-day widespread use of Arabic, Dutch, English, French, German, Italian, Portuguese, and Spanish.

Humanity gains so much from each fresh expression of itself in a language: 'The world is a mosaic of visions. With each language that disappears, a piece of that mosaic is lost.'[46] The best way for an educated person to feel the power of this argument, I always think, is to ask what would be missed if – through an imaginary catastrophic

[45] Grosjean (1982: vii, 2). See also Baker and Prys Jones (1998).
[46] Aryon Dall'Igna Rodrigues, reported in Geary (1997: 54).

language disappearance – we had never had X (where X is any well-known language). What splendours of literature, in particular, would we have never experienced if some event had prematurely ended the development of French, or Spanish, or Russian? What if Norman French had succeeded in displacing Old English after 1066? No Chaucer, Shakespeare, Wordsworth, Dickens now. What if French had never been? No Molière, Hugo, Baudelaire. It has become a cliché, but that does not diminish its truth, to say that everyone would be the poorer. And we already sense our poverty when we reflect on the limited corpus of written materials we have available from the classical periods of, say, Greece or Rome.

But this way of thinking can be transferred to all languages – whether they have achieved prominence on the world literary stage or not. Our focus is on those which have not. What would we lose by their disappearance? We only know from those cases where material has been compiled – but enough of these are now available to demonstrate the existence of that 'mosaic of visions'. There we find – even if only through the medium of translation and second-hand telling – arrays of memorable characters and ingenious plots, reflections on the human condition, imaginative descriptions, and virtually unlimited creative manipulations of language. Every language, it would seem, has its Chaucer. In one collection of North American Indian tales, for example, there is a narrative about Coyote, the most powerful of the animal people, and how he defeated the monsters of the Bitterroot Valley, in western Montana.[47] It is a fine tale full of

---

[47] In Edmonds and Clark (1989: 20–3).

the humour, bravura, and timeless surrealism of folklore, with vividly drawn landscapes, larger-than-life personalities, and lively conversational exchanges. We happen to know of this story, because ethnologist Ella E. Clark went and transcribed it, in the summer of 1955, from a great-great-grandmother living on the Flathead Reservation – the only person there, it seems, who knew any of the old stories. The particular Salishan language she used is dead now. If the task had been left a few years, we would not have been able to share that story. We shall never know what stories delighted the Kasabe (see p. 1).[48]

One story does not make a world view. A world view gradually emerges through the accumulation of many sources from a community – its myths and legends, its accounts of traditions and practices, and a vast amount of cultural knowledge which is all too inadequately summed up by the single word 'heritage'. It is so easy to underestimate the detailed nature of this knowledge. But all over the world, encounters with indigenous peoples bring to light a profound awareness of fauna and flora, rocks and soils, climatic cycles and their impact on the land, the interpretation of landscape, and the whole question of the balance of natural forces (what above we called 'ecology'). Most Westerners are infants in their knowledge of the environment, and of how to behave towards it, compared with indigenous peoples, for whom the environment is

---

[48] An anecdote reported by the Dauenhauers (1998: 96) deserves repeating: Jewish writer Isaac Singer was once asked in an interview why he wrote in Yiddish, as it was a dying language. 'So I like ghost stories', Singer replied. 'Also, I believe in the resurrection. What will all those Jews have to read when they come back to life if I don't write in Yiddish?'

part of the business of survival. Their holistic thinking integrates concepts of environmental sustainability with concepts of community wellbeing and individual health. And it is precisely because there is this closeness of relationship between the people and their environment that there is such a 'mosaic of visions'. Having spread throughout the globe, indigenous communities have developed a hugely diverse set of responses in lifestyle, as they relate and react to the many differences in local environmental conditions. And it is language that unifies everything, linking environmental practice with cultural knowledge, and transmitting everything synchronically among the members of a community, as well as diachronically between generations.

World views are all-encompassing notions; so, to obtain a sense of what an indigenous world view is requires enormous commitment from an outsider – at the very least, sharing the life of the people to a degree, and taking on board the responsibilities which inevitably follow. There are few reports which do justice to the shared experience, though one which must come close is F. David Peat's book about his time with the Blackfoot.[49] A theoretical physicist, his account has an inclusiveness of subject-matter which is often missing in ethnological reports, in that his scientific background motivates him to reflect on a broader set of questions than is usual, ranging from boat construction to quantum physics. The coverage of his book is worth quoting at length, as it draws attention to the many elements that form part of the world view we must expect to encounter in an

---

[49] Peat (1995: xi).

indigenous setting. It is light years away from the regrettably still widespread misconceptions about the 'limited'
abilities of 'primitive' peoples.

Within the chapters of this book can be found discussions
of metaphysics and philosophy; the nature of space and time;
the connection between language, thought, and perception;
mathematics and its relationship to time; the ultimate nature
of reality; causality and interconnection; astronomy and the
movements of time; healing; the inner nature of animals, rocks,
and plants; powers of animation; the importance of maintaining
a balanced exchange of energy; of agriculture; of genetics; of
considerations of ecology; of the connection of the human
being to the cosmos; and of the nature of processes of knowing.
In addition, there are references to technologies such as the
Clovis spear point, ocean-going vessels and birchbark canoes,
tepees and longhouses, the development of corn and other
plants, farming methods, observational astronomy and record
keeping, and the preparation of medicines from various
sources.

Throughout his book, Peat draws attention to the parallels
he has found between Western and indigenous ways of
thinking, and explores the insights that can come from
comparing the different perspectives. To take just three
of these. Western ecologists emphasize the interconnect-
edness of nature; so do indigenous peoples, who have
identified connections unknown to Western science.
Many Western physicians have come to supplement the
traditional medical model with insights to do with the
relationship between body and mind – a view traditionally
held by indigenous healers, who have never fragmented
their vision of health. And several Western physicists are
developing a conception of nature, not as a collection of

objects in interaction but as a flux of processes; again, the notion of flux and process, Peat demonstrates, is fundamental to the indigenous world view which he is reporting.

But what is the role of language, in all of this? It is in fact pervasive. Many statements testify to the way a community's elders, leaders, and educators explicitly acknowledge the importance of their language as an expression of their whole society and history. They see language as the means of transmitting the story of the great journeys, wars, alliances, and apocalyptic events of their past; it is the chief mechanism of their rituals; it is the means of conveying ancient myths and legends, and their beliefs about the spirit world, to new generations; it is a way of expressing their network of social relationships; and it provides an ongoing commentary on their interaction with the landscape. As a result, Westerners wishing to learn from the indigenous experience find they have to rely on language for virtually everything. And there are now many reports, from different parts of the world, of the kind of 'discovery' which can be made by investigators who take a language seriously, and use it as a guide to understanding a community's world view. Animal management, agriculture, botany, and medicine are some of the areas where language has directed and interpreted observation in ways which have proved to be far more efficient and fruitful than traditional methods of empirical observation. For example, in the botanical domain, it is possible for Western observers to look at two plants and see no obvious difference between them; reference to the local language, however, shows that the plants have been given different names, thus suggesting a difference in species or ecological function.

Nicholas Evans, working on Australian aboriginal languages, reports several instances from zoological and botanical domains.[50] There are cases of animal and plant species which had distinct names in Aboriginal languages long before they came to be recognized as species within Western biological taxonomy. There is a species of python, for example, given a Western name only in the 1960s (*Morelia oenpelliensis*), which had long been recognized by the name *nawaran* in Kunwinjku (also spelled Gunwinggu, spoken in parts of northern Australia). That language also has a range of vocabulary which not only identifies male, female, and juvenile kangaroos, in their different species (*Macropus: antilopinus / bernardus / robustus / agilis*), but also describes their different manners of hopping. Evans points out that recent computer vision programs devised by zoologists to identify wallaby species have had more success when focusing on movement than on static appearance – something the Kunwinjku have known for generations. Likewise, various features of the network of ecological relationships recognized by the community can be disclosed through the events reported in its stories, as well as in the way its lexicon is organized. Evans gives an example from Mparntwe Arrernte (an Australian language spoken around Alice Springs), whose vocabulary provides different names for grubs (an important food source) according to the types of bush where they are found.

Other domains present similar opportunities. Insight into the various plant species used by indigenous healers may come from the way they are named and described in

[50] Evans (1998: 163–4).

ritual practices, formal oratory, or folktale.[51] The network of social relations within a community can most efficiently be understood by examining the rules governing the style of language used, the selection of vocabulary, and the choice of one manner of discourse rather than another. And it is even possible to obtain clues about the early history (or pre-history) of a community by examining the way it uses language; a contrast encoded in vocabulary may be enough to suggest a former behavioural reality for which archaeologists might then find evidence. The genetic relationships found between languages may also cast light on the early movements and groupings of peoples.[52]

World art as well as science can gain from the encounter with indigenous communities, which provide a source of new art forms that have often been used as inspiration by Western painters, sculptors, craft workers, and decorative artists. Language can be central to the appreciation of these forms, as they commonly represent a mythological or folkloric tradition which needs verbal elaboration if it is to be understood. The dreamings of Aboriginal Australia provide a well-studied example.[53] In the case of the verbal arts – a notion that subsumes a large array of genres, such as poetry, folktale, nursery rhyme, oration, song, and chant – the focus is, self-evidently, on the forms of the

[51] Fiona Archer, an ethnobotanist working in the Richtersveld region of north-eastern South Africa, where Khoisan languages are still spoken, has identified the names of some 120 plant species used by traditional healers, whose uses include acting as a general health tonic and skin protection. Report by Koch and Maslamoney (1997: 29).

[52] The relationship between genetic linguistic thinking and archaeology is illustrated in Adelaar (1998: 3).

[53] The combination of artistic form and linguistic commentary is well illustrated in Ebes and Hollow (1992).

language itself. One of the great successes of ethnolin-
guistics has been to draw attention to the distinctive
and elaborate ways in which different languages weave
patterns of sound, grammar, vocabulary, idiom, and figurative expression as part of their conventions of artistic
discourse.[54] Anyone who has enjoyed the use of repetitive
sound (alliteration, assonance, rhyme) in Western poetry
will not fail to be impressed by the exploitation of these
devices in indigenous languages. And anyone who has
had to cope with the demands of speech-genre differences
in their own lives, either as producers or listeners (after-
dinner speeches, votes of thanks, funeral orations, wel-
coming addresses, party recitations), knows how difficult
it is to master the linguistic techniques required to make
the language elegant and effective. It is a salutary experience, then, to encounter the oratorical range, technical
complexity, and communicative power displayed by the
master speakers of indigenous languages.

The potential for discovery through language is still
considerable. It should not be forgotten that, despite all
the dangers that indigenous peoples are facing, they are
still responsible for around a fifth of the surface of the
earth. As Darrell Posey puts it: they are 'active stewards of
some of the most biologically and ecologically rich
regions of the world'.[55] Doubtless there will be relatively
few dramatic moments, in the ongoing process of linguistic enquiry – there are, after all, 'only' a few thousand
possibilities, and as many of these languages are members

---

[54] A wide range of genres is illustrated in Bauman and Sherzer (1974); see
also the examples in Crystal (1997a: 49, 60).

[55] Posey (1997: 8).

of closely related families (and thus displaying a great deal of similarity to each other), not all linguistic investigations will give rise to exciting new insights. But, in principle, each language provides a new slant on how the human mind works, and how it expresses itself in linguistic categories: 'Language embodies the intellectual wealth of the people who use it.'[56]

A statement of this kind allows me to return to the general perspective which opened this section, where the emphasis was on all languages – not just the less well-known ones (to Western minds) which I have been calling 'indigenous'. The context of this book demands a special focus on those languages which are most endangered, but the rhetoric of the present section requires that we adopt an appropriately universal viewpoint. It is every language that we are talking about – English and French alongside Kunwinjku and Mparntwe Arrernte. It is every dialect of every language that we are talking about. It is every emerging form of every language that we are talking about. When it comes to appreciating the power of the human language faculty, as a source of knowledge, insight, and wisdom, the traditional nomenclature – language, dialect, creole, pidgin, patois, vernacular, koiné, lingo, etc. – ceases to be relevant; for any speech system, whether viewed by a society as prestigious or humble, educated or ignorant, pleasant or ugly, is capable of telling us something we did not know before. Several leading twentieth-century writers have remarked on the value of knowing other languages – or at least, the translated products of other languages. T. S. Eliot had this to say:[57]

---

[56] Hale (1992b: 36).   [57] Eliot (1942/1953: 234).

We are greatly helped to develop objectivity of taste if we can appreciate the work of foreign authors, living in the same world as ourselves, and expressing their vision of it in another great language.

The word 'great' is superfluous, for all languages have authors, as we have seen, who are in the business of expressing a vision. (Or perhaps we should leave it in – as long as we understand by it that all languages are great.) A similar alteration needs to be made to Rudyard Kipling's observation:[58]

The reason why one has to parse and construe and grind at the dead tongues in which certain ideas are expressed, is *not* for the sake of what is called intellectual training – that may be given in other ways – but because only in that tongue is that idea expressed with absolute perfection.

Whatever the term 'perfection' means, it applies to all languages, and not just the dead classical tongues. But the spirit of these observations, drawing attention to the uniqueness of individual languages, is very much in tune with my argument, as is this comment by Ezra Pound:[59]

The sum of human wisdom is not contained in any one language, and no single language is capable of expressing all forms and degrees of human comprehension.

So, one way of increasing our stock of human wisdom is to learn more languages, and to learn more about languages. And one way of ensuring that this sum of human wisdom is made available – if not for ourselves, then for the benefit of future generations – is to do as much as we

---

[58] Kipling (1912/1928: 85).   [59] Pound (1960: ch. 1).

can to preserve them now, at a time when they seem to be most in danger. This argument is developed in chapter 4. For the present, I simply assert that, as each language dies, another precious source of data – for philosophers, scientists, anthropologists, folklorists, historians, psychologists, linguists, writers – is lost. With only some 6,000 sources in all, the word 'precious' is not being used lightly. Nor are such words as 'tragedy', in the following remarks by one of America's leading field linguists, Ken Hale:[60]

In this circumstance [the embodiment of intellectual wealth in language], there is a certain tragedy for the human purpose. The loss of local languages, and of the cultural systems that they express, has meant irretrievable loss of diverse and interesting intellectual wealth, the priceless products of human mental industry.

Diversity, as we have seen, is a human evolutionary strength, and should be safeguarded as an end in itself, for out of it new 'houses of being' can spring.[61] Moreover, diversity breeds diversity – as we have seen in Western encounters with the artistic traditions of other cultures, which have led to new movements, trends, and fashions in one's own. Nor should we forget the literary perspective. As George Steiner reminds us:[62]

Is it not the duty of the critic to avail himself, in some imperfect measure at least, of another language – if only to experience the defining contours of his own?

[60] Hale (1992b: 36).
[61] The metaphor is Heidegger's: 'Language is the house of being.' See the 'Letter on humanism' (1947), discussed in Heidegger (1971: 135).
[62] 'F. R. Leavis', in Steiner (1967: 264).

In the final section of this chapter, I illustrate what some of these contours are.

Because languages are interesting in themselves

This is my fifth and final answer to the question 'Why should we care about language death?' If you find the word 'interesting' too weak, then replace it by 'fascinating', 'useful', 'important', or some other more powerful adjective, in the light of the other four reasons above. But in this section, I want to sidestep issues to do with world resources, sociopolitical identity, personal relationships, and other such matters of moment, and concentrate solely on language, seen as the subject-matter of linguistics, a branch of human knowledge in its own right.

The aim of linguistics is to define the nature of the human language faculty, comprehensively and explicitly. What is the range of possibilities which the human brain allows, when it comes to the construction of languages? To answer this question, we need to obtain evidence from as many languages as we can, and to go back as far into history (and pre-history) as we can. Each language manifests a fresh coming-together of sounds, grammar, and vocabulary to form a system of communication which, while demonstrating certain universal principles of organization and structure, is an unprecedented event and a unique encapsulation of a world view.[63]

---

[63] The spirits of Benjamin Lee Whorf and Edward Sapir have been present throughout much of this chapter. The Sapir–Whorf hypothesis combined two principles: *linguistic determinism* (our language determines the way we think) and *linguistic relativity* (the distinctions

The more languages we study, the fuller our picture of the human linguistic options will be. Languages which are 'off the beaten track' are especially important, as their isolation means that they may have developed features not found in other languages.[64] And language death is the chief threat to the achievement of this goal as, with the death of each language, another source of potentially invaluable information disappears.

This point is usually a source of surprise to people who have not carried out some study of linguistics: the fact that indigenous communities have languages which are as full and complex as English or French is simply not widely known, and traditional Western belief assumes the contrary. Early colonial contempt for subjugated peoples was automatically transferred to their languages, which would be described as rudimentary or animal-like. This was reinforced by the perceived primitiveness of a community's

encoded in one language are not found in any other). Nothing in this book requires us to accept the deterministic form of this hypothesis: it is perfectly possible, through translation, bilingual paraphrase, and other techniques, to comprehend at least some of the thought processes in speakers of other languages. The examples on pp. 75ff. are different from English, but are not thereby incomprehensible. With linguistic relativity, differences between languages are recognized, but are not considered insurmountable. For Whorf's original views, see J. B. Carroll (1956), especially Whorf's paper, 'Science and linguistics'. For a discussion, see Gumperz and Levinson (1996).

[64] It is sometimes forgotten just how linguistically diverse certain parts of the world are. Europe is not a typical place. Indo-European, with its familiar groupings of Germanic, Celtic, Romance, Slavic, and so on, has only a dozen families. By contrast, there are over fifty families in North America, some consisting of many languages, others of just single languages (isolates), and twice as many in South America. These languages are as different from each other as, say, English is from Welsh, French, or Russian, if not more so.

culture or technology, by comparison with Western standards; it was – and still is – widely believed that a culture which is technologically primitive cannot possibly have a richly complex language. Marianne Mithun, a specialist in North American indigenous languages, is one who firmly states the reality:[65]

There is not a language in North America that fails to offer breathtakingly beautiful intricacy. For descendants of speakers to discover this beauty can profoundly enrich their lives, much like the discovery of music, literature, or art, if not more.

Despite such statements, which abound in the anthropological and linguistic literature, it is horrifyingly common to encounter the view, among people who in other respects are well educated, that aboriginal languages are undeveloped, containing only a few hundred words or no abstract words at all, or that there are peoples whose languages are so basic that they have to resort to signs to express their needs. Unfortunately, this mindset is so well established in Western culture that it is a serious hindrance to progress in eliciting support for endangered languages. After all, the argument goes, if an indigenous language is so primitive, it is hardly any loss. So it needs to be categorically stated, at every opportunity, that this view is demonstrable nonsense (see also fn. 7 above). And that means providing examples to make the demonstration.

The demonstration can relate to any aspect of language structure – phonology (pronunciation), grammar, vocabulary, discourse. I shall give brief examples from each of these areas, related where possible to English. First,

---

[65] Mithun (1998: 189).

phonology. The languages of the world widely diverge from the kind of sound system we find in English (which, depending on the accent, has about 44 vowels and consonants). One of the features of Ubykh (p. 2) which fascinated linguists was its large consonant inventory – 80 consonants – over three times as many as in English 'received pronunciation', which has 24. This numerical fact alone should be enough to quash the myth that indigenous languages have a 'primitive' structure. But from a linguistic point of view, there are more interesting comparisons to be made: within the 24 English consonants, great use is made of contrasts in vocal cord vibration ('voiced' vs 'voiceless' sounds, such as the initial sounds of *bin* vs *pin* or *van* vs *fan*), and more use is made of fricative sounds than of any other type (the initial sounds of *fat, vat, thin, this, see, zoo, shoe, hat,* and the final sound in *beige*); by contrast, Australian Aboriginal languages make hardly any use of the voicing contrast, and fricatives are conspicuous by their absence.[66] That there could be languages without fricatives was a real surprise when they were first encountered.

A particularly important finding relates to the Khoisan language family of southern Africa, which is the only family to display so many complex systems of click consonants (the kinds of sound which are heard on the margins of English, in such vocalizations as *tut tut*). When European explorers first encountered these languages, clicks were so alien to their ears that the speech was readily dismissed as bizarre and animal-like – compared to the clucking of hens or the gobbling of turkeys. But no

---

[66] Yallop (1982: ch. 3).

set of animal noises could even remotely resemble the system of phonological contrasts found in, for example, !Xu, which in one analysis has 48 distinct click sounds.[67] And the point needs to be made: if Khoisan languages had all died out before linguists had described them, it is unlikely that we would ever have guessed that human beings would use such an apparently minor feature of sound production to such complex effect.

Differences in the way languages use grammar are always illuminating, especially those which help to quash the myth of primitiveness in indigenous languages. There are many languages which provide ways of expressing an area of experience that actually offer more points of contrastivity than are available in languages like English or French. The lack of such contrasts may even be felt, by English speakers, when we find it necessary to add extra words to explain our point, or find ourselves in danger of ambiguity.

Here are some of the possibilities in the system of English personal pronouns, where we make the following distinctions:

1st person singular	*I*	1st person plural	*we*
2nd person singular	*you*	2nd person plural	*you*
3rd person singular	*he / she / it*	3rd person plural	*they*

It is easy to see that there are several possible contrasts which this system cannot express, and several ambiguities which can and do arise. If I use *you*, when talking to several people, it may not be clear whether I mean 'one

---

[67] Maddieson (1984: 422), reproduced in Crystal (1997a: 170). The exclamation mark represents one of these clicks.

of you', 'two of you', or 'all of you'. If I use *we* with a group of people, it may not be clear whether I mean 'two of us', 'a sub-group of us', or 'all of us'. In addition, there are problems in adapting the system to cope with socio-linguistic change: we have a sex-neutral 3rd person plural, but no sex-neutral 3rd person singular, so in these days of equality we are constantly being faced with the awkward-ness of such forms as *he and she* (or *she and he*), and inventions of a new sex-neutral pronoun are regularly proposed.[68]

All of these 'missing' distinctions, along with several others, can be found distributed among the pronoun systems of the world's languages. Many languages have a neutral 3rd person singular pronoun; many have *dual* pronouns, expressing the notions of 'we two', 'you two', or 'they two'; many permit speakers to distinguish between 1st person inclusive ('you and I') and 1st person exclusive ('we two but not you'). Some languages (e.g. Nunggubuyu, Australia) have pronouns distinguishing 'you two [male]' and 'you two [female]' or 'we two [male]' and 'we two [female]'; some (e.g. Aneityum, Vanuatu) have *trial* pronouns, allowing the speaker to distinguish between 'we two', 'we three', and 'we many'; some (e.g. Cree, Canada) have a fourth person, allowing the distinc-tion between 'him' and 'another man apart from him'.[69] The English-derived pidgin language, Tok Pisin (Papua New Guinea), operates a basic six-term system as follows:

---

[68] Several of these proposals are listed in Crystal (1997a: 46).
[69] Several pronoun systems are described in Bloomfield (1933: 252 ff.). For Australian Aboriginal pronouns, see Yallop (1982: 73 ff.). The Tok Pisin system is illustrated in Todd (1984: 192 ff.).

mi	I	*yumi*	we (inclusive – you and me)
yu	you	*mipela*	we (exclusive – we not you)
em	he she it	*ol*	they

But this system can then be expanded to produce such forms as:

mitupela	the two of us (but not you)
mitripela	the three of us (but not you)
yumitripela	the three of us (including you)
yutupela	the two of you
emtripela	the three of them
yumifoapela	the four of us (including you)

At least pronoun systems have a familiar correlative in a language like English. However, several of the grammatical features found in indigenous languages present us with ways of talking about the world that have no counterpart in the well-known Western languages. In English, if I make an observation such as 'The book fell on the floor', there is nothing in the sentence to tell the listener whether I saw this happen myself or whether the sentence is reporting what I have heard from someone else. In some languages, this distinction is encoded within the verb phrase, so that one *must* choose between forms which say whether one is an eye-witness or not. Because the language is expressing the kind of evidence involved, the grammatical system has been called *evidentiality*.[70]

---

[70] For other examples of grammatical differences, see Dixon (1998: 117–27). There is a general discussion of evidentiality in Palmer (1986: 66 ff.), and a wide range of illustrations from different languages in Chafe and Nichols (1986). For the original account of Tuyuca, see Barnes (1984).

In Ngiyambaa (Australia), for example, one would distinguish these two sentences:

ngindu gara garambiyi   ngindu dhan garambiyi
'one can see you were sick'   'you are said to have been sick'

The first form expresses sensory evidence; the second expresses reported, linguistic evidence. In Tuyuca (Brazil and Colombia), a system of five evidentials is reported:

Visual   *diiga ape-wi*
             'I saw him play soccer'
Non-visual   *diiga ape-ti*
             'I heard the game and him, but I didn't see it
             or him'
Apparent   *diiga ape-yi*
             'I have seen evidence that he played soccer –
             such as his clothes in the changing room – but
             I did not see him play'
Secondhand   *diiga ape-yigi*
             'I obtained the information that he played
             soccer from someone else'
Assumed   *diiga ape-hiyi*
             'It is reasonable to assume that he played soccer'

The basic translation of each of these sentences is the same: 'He played soccer.' But in addition to the core meaning, each sentence gives an additional slant. And the important point to appreciate is that it is not possible to produce a sentence without expressing one or other of these slants. We must, in effect, always be answering an imaginary question: 'What is the evidence on which you based your statement?'

Evidentiality systems take some getting used to, because their way of dealing with the expression of truth is so unlike the way in which speakers of English (amongst many others) approach the world. Dixon, reflecting on this point, observes:[71]

Wouldn't it be wonderful if there was obligatory specification of evidence in English? Think how much easier the job of a policeman would be. And how it would make politicians be more honest about the state of the national budget.

Why evidentials should develop in one language, or group of languages, rather than another, is of course a fascinating – though currently unanswerable – question. But the key point, for the present book, is to note the challenge it presents to our own way of thinking. It is likely that few of us – unless we have a background in linguistics (or, of course, have learned one of the languages which display it) – will have encountered an evidential system before. Having done so, it undoubtedly adds a new dimension to our conception of how verbs can operate in human sentences. Our picture of language has become fuller, as a result. The thought that we might never have learned about this way of organizing sentence meaning, because the languages might have died before we could study them, we can put out of our minds. The job has been done. Then another thought comes creeping back: what other such discoveries will never be made, because the languages that display them will be dead before we get a chance to record them?

Vocabulary is the third main area of illustration, when demonstrating the kinds of illumination that can come from comparative linguistic studies. Here, most of the

---

[71] Dixon (1998: 120).

examples work by comparing the *words* which a language makes available to talk about a particular area of experience.[72] The assumption is that if a language has a word for an entity (rather than a circumlocution of some kind), this says something about the place of that entity within the culture. Distinctions encoded in words are taken to represent important cultural perceptions and needs. Some of the contrasts are inevitably rather obvious and trivial: for example, it is hardly surprising to note that European languages have many words for types of motor vehicle whereas Brazilian rainforest languages do not. We must also distinguish fact from fiction: the mythical number of words for 'snow' in Eskimo falls into this category.[73]

[72] Technically, *lexemes*: for this notion, see Crystal (1997a: 104 ff.). It is important to appreciate that the semantic units of a language do not always correspond to the way speech operates with separate words, or represents them in writing. A *flowerpot* is a semantic unit, whether it is written *flower pot* or *flower-pot*; *switch on* is a semantic unit (a 'phrasal verb') despite its two words; and *take, takes, taking, taken*, and *took* are all forms of a single semantic unit. This last point is especially relevant, when addressing such topics as 'language X has hundreds of words for ...': the 'hundreds' may only be the result of lots of case endings applied to a relatively few words. This is one of the misconceptions behind the 'words for snow in Eskimo' myth: see fn. 73.

[73] An early anthropological curiosity over whether Inuit (Eskimo) languages had a general term covering *all* kinds of snow led to periods of speculation about just how many words the language had for *different* kinds of snow. Various totals have been proposed, ranging from tens to hundreds. The question is really unanswerable in any simple way, as it depends on which words count as belonging to the 'snow' field, whether a sequence of forms is a compound word or not, whether there are dialect differences, and other considerations. In one account, Anthony Woodbury identifies words in Yup'ik Eskimo which name five types of snow particle, five types of fallen snow, three types of snow formation, and two types of snowy weather conditions. This total (15) sounds impressive, until we consider the list of words in English for the same semantic field: these include *sleet, slush, snow, flurry, dusting, powder,*

Rather more interesting are those cases where the area of cultural experience is shared between widely different languages – as in the case of kinship relations.

Kinship terms include such words as *mother*, *father*, *uncle*, *aunt*, *son*, *daughter*, and *cousin*. European languages display some differences – French, for example, expresses the difference between male and female cousins (*cousin/ cousine*), whereas in English it is not possible to tell just by hearing the word which sex your cousin is. English does not have a large kinship vocabulary, and some of its limitations can cause problems. We have to resort to circumlocutions such as 'uncle on your mother's side', because there are no single words to express such distinctions as 'mother's brother' vs 'father's brother' or 'mother's sister' vs 'father's sister'. 'Older' and 'younger' brothers and sisters cannot be easily distinguished: if you have one 'older brother', there is no difficulty in describing him, but if you have more than one, it is not always easy to express the difference between them ('this is the second youngest of my four younger brothers'). A 'brother's wife's father' cannot be referred to in any simple way. When it gets as far as 'second' vs 'third' cousins or the world of people who are 'once removed', 'twice removed', and so on, most people give up trying to understand. The 'in-law' relationship can be especially difficult. Is the brother of your father-in-law your 'uncle-in-law'? Does he count as an uncle at all?

---

avalanche, blizzard, drift, snowflake, snowstorm, snowdrift, snowman, snowball, snowbank, snowbound, snowcap, snowfield, snowpack, snowscape, snowslip ... we could go on. For further discussion, see Martin (1986) and Pullum (1991).

Many indigenous languages, by contrast, have vocabularies of hundreds of words, plainly identifying the importance of familial relationships within their cultures, and handling relationships of this kind with ease, once the terms have been learned. These lexicons take into account major differences of social function – for example, whose responsibility it is to raise a child after the death of a parent, or who counts as a close relative and who does not. They help identify the roles played by the two sets of in-laws and the boundaries of the extended family. Different factors are influential – sex, age, blood, marriage, generation, and clan (a type of relationship in which people are seen as kin if they belong to a particular grouping within a tribe). Kinship is a good example of the way languages differ in the way they handle an area of human experience. The same biological relationships are involved everywhere, yet they are handled in a multiplicity of ways, reflecting the influence of cultural factors. Many Amerindian and Australian Aboriginal languages demonstrate highly sophisticated kinship systems, and have received a great deal of linguistic attention as a consequence.

The order of birth can be important: words for brothers and sisters may reflect distinctions of age, so that the 'older' vs 'younger' ambiguity is avoided. There may be full sets of vocabulary for in-laws. The word for 'father' may be used to refer to the father's brothers or even cousins – in other words, a set of men who are equivalent in terms of social status and responsibility. Similarly, their children may all be called 'brothers' and 'sisters'. There may be cyclical effects, the same term being applied to one's 'father's father' and to one's 'son's son' – for example, Pitjantjatjara *tjamu* means 'grandson' as well as 'grandfather'. Such languages have nothing comparable to the unilinear and unending progression of 'great-', 'great-great-', and so on, which we use in English. In Pintup there are words for various combinations of relatives, e.g. 'two brothers' or 'a father and his son'. And in Alyawarra, most of the dual and plural personal pronouns have three different forms, depending on which tribal grouping the addressees belong to. All three of the following forms mean 'you two', but the reference is different each time:

mpula – used to members of the same narrow group within the tribe[74]

mpulaka – used to people who are not members of the same narrow group, but of the same broader group

mpulantha – used to members of different broader groups.

Language may also express kinship relationships in other ways than vocabulary: whole styles of speech may change as a result of taboo relationships which are brought into existence following marriage or death. Much discussed is the case of the 'avoidance languages' found in Australia. It is common for a man to avoid several of his wife's relatives – usually his wife's mother and brothers, sometimes his wife's father and sisters. Avoidance means different things, ranging from complete physical avoidance to permitted address using a special language. Dixon's classic study of the avoidance situation in Dyirbal drew

---

[74] I am avoiding the use of technical anthropological terminology here: *section, subsection, patrimoiety.* For an exposition, in the context of Australian languages, see Yallop (1982: 152 ff.).

attention to the linguistic option.[75] There the everyday language is called Guwal, while the 'mother-in-law' language is called Dyalnguy, used to address other persons whenever a taboo relative was within earshot. The differences are almost entirely lexical, with Dyalnguy having a vocabulary about a quarter of the size of Guwal.

Vocabulary, grammar, and phonology have been the chief dimensions of enquiry, when linguists try to identify the range, complexity, and limitations of the human language faculty. Other factors, to do with such matters as patterns of discourse, pragmatic choice, and stylistic variation, have also been taken into account. In most cases, of course, the enquiry raises issues which go beyond the strictly linguistic: kinship vocabulary leads to a consideration of social relationships; evidential sentence patterns lead to reflections about the way a society views truth. For the linguist, the primary task is to describe as fully and as accurately as possible what the languages are doing, in terms which will facilitate cross-linguistic comparison. Ultimately, the aim is to be fully explicit in specifying all the variables involved, so that we can answer with some confidence the question 'what form can a human language take?' This question provides theoretical linguistics with its focus, and techniques of formulating the best kind of

---

[75] Dixon (1972). Another example of a unique discourse style in Australian languages is Damin, learned as part of a man's initiation among the Lardil of North Queensland. Damin has a sound system which is very different from Lardil, and a hugely reduced vocabulary which is constructed in such a way that, according to Ken Hale, it can express virtually any idea yet be learned in a day, using a system of abstract names for logically cohesive families of concepts. The last fluent user of Damin died some years ago. See Hale (1998: 205 ff.).

answer have been the preoccupation of that subject in recent decades. In a world with only one language, it is sobering to realize just how far from the truth our answer would be. And with languages continuing to die unstudied, we find our linguistic vision steadily narrowing, and the possibilities of a comprehensive answer moving frustratingly further and further away.

The mental challenge of constructing grammars whose abstract formulations are capable of handling the multitude of similarities and differences among languages has attracted some of the best linguistic minds. But this has its down side. The search for universals of language has resulted in a significant expenditure of energy on the real or imagined underlying similarities between languages, with little left to focus on linguistic differences. It is now possible to carry on a successful career in linguistics without ever having done any descriptive work on a language – let alone on an endangered language. When I worked in the linguistics department of the University of Reading, between the 1960s and 1980s, it was standard practice to train students in basic field linguistics, using as input the languages spoken by informants who were attending the university for other reasons (such as studying a course in agriculture). The constraints of the course meant that it was never possible to spend more than 20 or 30 hours on a language, but a lot can be done in that time, and it did provide a close encounter with the realities of descriptive work, which are often a lot messier than theoreticians like to admit. None of this was comparable to the kind of exposure encountered in real fieldwork abroad, but it was a move in the right direction. What is to be regretted is that not more of this kind of work is being done.

The point has been strongly made by Dixon, who has got his feet dirty in the field more than most. Of all the kinds of linguistic work he has undertaken, undertaking the analysis of a previously undescribed language is, for him, 'the toughest task in linguistics', yet 'the most exciting and the most satisfying of work'. He conveys this in a paragraph which deserves to be quoted in full:[76]

It is hard to convey the sheer mental exhilaration of field work on a new language. First, one has to recognise the significant analytic problems. Then alternative solutions may tumble around in one's head all night. At the crack of dawn one writes them down, the pros and cons of each. During the day it is possible to assess the alternatives, by checking back through texts that have already been gathered and by asking carefully crafted questions of native speakers. One solution is seen to be clearly correct – it is simpler than the others, and has greater explanatory power. Then one realises that the solution to this problem sheds light on another knotty conundrum that has been causing worry for weeks. And so on.

But later in his book, he draws attention to the problem:

The most important task in linguistics today – indeed, the only really important task – is to get out in the field and describe languages, while this can still be done ... If every linguistics student (and faculty member) in the world today worked on just one language that is in need of study, the prospects for full

---

[76] Dixon (1997: 134); quotations below are from pp. 137 and 144. For similar views, see Krauss (1998: 108–9) and Grinevald (1998: 154–5). There have, incidentally, been several cases reported of students applying to do research on endangered languages being turned down by a linguistics department on the grounds that their proposals were of insufficient theoretical interest.

documentation of endangered languages (before they fade away) would be rosy. I doubt if one linguist in twenty is doing this.

The implications of this are very serious, and will be addressed at the end of chapter 5.

Conclusion

I know there are many people on this planet who cannot stand the thought of difference, or of people with different identities from their own, and who go out of their way to reject, attack, and oppress them. The newspapers are full of examples of nationalist and racist antagonisms and hatreds. The arguments of this chapter will regrettably have no appeal to those who think in this way. But there are also many people who maintain a belief in human equality, who condemn discrimination, who are worried by the global trend towards standardization, who are concerned about ecological issues, and who delight in cultural diversity. These people are as interested in others because of their cultural differences as because of their similarities. They know that growth in their depth of perception about what it means to be human is enhanced by knowledge about those who think and act in a different way. They would accept Hamlet's accusation: 'There are more things in heaven and earth, Horatio, / Than are dreamt of in your philosophy' (I.v.166).

What is so puzzling is why so many of this world's Horatios are unaware of the facts and arguments surrounding language death. For they are indeed many – and (to anticipate one of the arguments of chapter 5) many means money. As we shall see, there are several things which can be done to help alleviate the situation, but they all cost. And whether the cost is met by governments or by private support of charitable agencies, the underlying message is the same: only a vast sea-change in popular attitude will have the required impact, whether through the vote or through the cheque-book. But people need facts and arguments to motivate any such change. They need to believe, really believe, that language is 'the most valuable single possession of the human race'.[77] Hence the need for books such as the present one, for media presentations, and for such organizations as those referred to in the Appendix. In the final analysis, it is all to do with what we believe to be the important things in life. As one fieldworker has put it: 'To fight to preserve the smaller cultures and languages may turn out to be the struggle to preserve the most precious things that make us human before we end up in the land fill of history.'[78]

[77] Hockett (1958: ch. 1, line 1).   [78] Crow (1997: 4).

3

Why do languages die?

~

If people care about endangered languages, they will want
something to be done. But before we can decide what can
or should be done, we need to understand the reasons
for the endangerment in the first place. Why, then, are
languages dying, and in such numbers? And is the rate of
language death increasing?

Languages have always died. As cultures have risen and
fallen, so their languages have emerged and disappeared.
We can get some sense of it following the appearance of
written language, for we now have records (in various
forms – inscriptions, clay tablets, documents) of dozens
of extinct languages from classical times – Bithynian,
Cilician, Pisidian, Phrygian, Paphlagonian, Etruscan,
Sumerian, Elamite, Hittite ... We know of some 75
extinct languages which have been spoken in Europe
and Asia Minor.[1] But the extinct languages of which we
have some historical record in this part of the world must
be only a fraction of those for which we have nothing.
And when we extend our coverage to the whole world,
where written records of ancient languages are largely
absent, it is easy to see that no sensible estimate can be
obtained about the rate at which languages have died in
the past. We can of course make guesses at the size of the

---

[1] This is the total of asterisked items in these parts of the world as listed in
Voegelin and Voegelin (1977).

population in previous eras, and the likely size of communities, and (on the assumption that each community would have had its own language) work out possible numbers of languages. On this basis, Michael Krauss hazards that 10,000 years ago, assuming a world population of 5–10 million and an average community size of 500–1,000, there must have been between 5,000 and 20,000 languages.[2] He opts for 12,000 as a middle estimate of the highest number of languages in the world at any one time. There are some 6,000 languages now. But no one knows how many languages have come and gone within this period, and how many new languages to allow for, to set off against the apparent loss of some 6,000. Nor do we know whether the rate of language change has been constant over these long periods of time, or punctuated by periods of rapid shift and decline, though the topic has been much debated.[3]

There are very few historical records about world language use, apart from those collected during the period of European colonial expansion, and most of them are sporadic, inconsistent, and impressionistic. Rather more systematic material began to be accumulated with the development of comparative philology and the availability of population census data in the nineteenth century, and the rise of anthropology and linguistics in the twentieth; but even the latter subject did not make much headway with large-scale scientific surveys until the last quarter of that century. The widespread view that language death is rapidly increasing is based largely on general reasoning: for example, we know that there has been a significant

[2] Krauss (1998: 105).   [3] This is the central theme of Dixon (1997).

growth in the nation-state in the twentieth century, with an associated recognition of official languages; we know that there has been a significant growth in international and global lingua francas during the same period; and we can deduce that these developments will have put minority languages under increasing pressure. There are also some observer accounts and informant recollections, chiefly gathered since the 1960s, which allow us to quantify rate of decline; statistics about the numbers of speakers of different ages in different minority languages (such as those illustrated in chapter 1) would fall into this category. These, with just a few exceptions (see chapter 4), tend to show a steepening curve. But whether there is a real increase in rate or not, the comparative estimates that have been made of language families in various parts of the world tell the same story: the last 500 years have been a period of dramatic decline. For example, the number of languages spoken in Brazil in *c.* 1500 AD has been estimated to be about 1,175; today it is less than 200.[4]

It is not possible to come up with a single explanation for this decline; there are too many factors involved, variously combining in different regional situations: 'The search for a single cause which inevitably leads to language death is futile.'[5] Single-sentence answers to the 'why' question will often be heard, especially in the popular press (e.g. the current preoccupation with global English as '*the* cause' of language death), but they never do more than isolate one of the issues. The full range of factors is

---

[4] Rodrigues (1993). For other evidence of the recency of language shift, in particular communities, see England (1998: 105).
[5] Dorian (1981: 69).

fairly easy to identify, thanks to the many case studies which have now been made; what is impossible, in our current state of knowledge, is to generalize about them in global terms. The current situation is without precedent: the world has never had so many people in it, globalization processes have never been so marked; communication and transport technologies have never been so omnipresent; there has never been so much language contact; and no language has ever exercised so much international influence as English. How minority languages fare, in such an environment, is a matter of ongoing discovery. We are still at the stage of evaluating the role of these factors within individual countries – often, within restricted locations within countries. Trends are beginning to appear, but the limited database makes them tentative indeed. The following account, therefore, should not be taken as representing any order of precedence.

Factors which put the people in physical danger

Obviously, a language dies if all the people who speak it are dead; so any circumstance which is a direct and immediate threat to the physical safety of some or all of a community is, in a way, the bottom line. Many languages have become endangered, moribund, or extinct as a result of factors which have had a dramatic effect on the physical wellbeing of their speakers.

The number of a language's users can be seriously reduced, first of all, by catastrophic natural causes. Though accurate figures are virtually impossible to come by, it is evident that small communities in isolated areas can easily be decimated or wiped out by earthquakes, hurricanes, tsunamis, floods, volcanic eruptions, and other cataclysms. On 17 July 1998, a 7.1 (Richter) magnitude earthquake off the coast of E. Saundaun Province, Papua New Guinea, killed over 2,200 and displaced over 10,000: the villages of Sissano, Warupu, Arop, and Malol were destroyed; some 30% of the Arop and Warupu villagers were killed. The people in these villages had already been identified by Summer Institute of Linguistics researchers as being sufficiently different from each other in their speech to justify the recognition of four separate languages, but the matter was unresolved: according to *Ethnologue* (1996), surveys were needed in three cases; some work was in progress in the fourth. The numbers were already small: Sissano had only 4,776 in the 1990 census, Malol was estimated to have 3,330; Arop 1,700 in 1981; and Warupu 1,602 in 1983. The totals for Arup and Warupu will now each be at least 500 less. But as the villages were destroyed, and the survivors moved away to care centres and other locations, there must now be a real question-mark over whether these communities (and thus their languages) will survive the trauma of displacement.

Here we have an instance of the total destruction of a habitat. In other cases, the habitat may remain but become unsurvivable, through a combination of unfavourable climatic and economic conditions. Famine and drought are the two chief factors. The Irish potato famine (caused by the potato blights of 1845–6) resulted in 1 million deaths between 1845 and 1851 and the beginning of a long period of emigration; a population of 8 million in 1841 had become 6.5 million a decade later. The impact was greatest in rural communities, and as this was where Irish was chiefly spoken, the famine must have hastened the decline of Irish at the time.[6] In more recent times, especially in Africa, the statistics of famine, often compounded with the results of civil strife, carry an obvious implication for the languages spoken by the people most affected. In the 1983–5 Sahel drought in east and south Africa, UN agencies estimated that some 22 million were affected in over 20 countries. In the 1991–2 Somalia drought, a quarter of the children under the age of 5 died. In 1998, according to the UN World Food Programme, 10% of Sudan's 29-million population were at risk of starvation, chiefly in the south, the problem massively exacerbated by the ongoing civil war. The famine must already have seriously affected the fragile language totals found in several parts of the country. Of the 132 living languages listed for Sudan in *Ethnologue* (1996), there are estimates given for 122; of these, 17 were reported to have less than 1,000 speakers; 54 less than 10,000; and 105 less than 100,000.

The historical effect of imported disease on indigenous peoples is now well established, though the extraordinary scale of the effects, in the early colonial period, is still not widely appreciated.[7] Within 200 years of the arrival of the first Europeans in the Americas, it is thought that over 90% of the indigenous population was killed by the diseases which accompanied them, brought in by both

---

[6] For a historical account of the various factors contributing to the decline of Irish in the nineteenth century, see Edwards (1985: 53 ff.).

[7] See McNeill (1976), Stearn and Stearn (1945), Duffy (1953), Peat (1995: ch. 5). Several other parts of the world have a similar history: there were smallpox epidemics in South Africa in 1713, 1735, and 1767 (the Dutch landed at the Cape in 1652). See also Kinkade (1991: 157).

animals and humans. To take just one area: the Central Mexico population is believed to have been something over 25 million in 1518, when the Spanish arrived, but it had dropped to 1.6 million by 1620. Some estimates suggest that the population of the New World may have been as high as 100 million before European contact. Within 200 years this had dropped to less than 1 million. The scale of this disaster can only be appreciated by comparing it with others: it far exceeds the 25 million thought to have died from the Black Death in fourteenth-century Europe; it even well exceeds the combined total of deaths in the two World Wars (some 30–40 million).[8]

Less ferocious diseases can, nonetheless have a devastating effect on communities which have built up no resistance to them. There have been several reports of influenza, even the common [sic] cold, leading to the deaths of indigenous groups – a risk which must always prey on the minds of the aid workers, anthropologists, missionaries, linguists, and others who work with them. Disease has been identified as a critical factor in several cases: – for example, Andamanese (Pucikwar – down to 24 speakers in 1981).[9] AIDS, of course, is likely to have a

---

[8] Casualty figures from *The Cambridge encyclopedia*, 3rd edn (Crystal, 1997c). An estimate for the greater Amazonian region suggests that it contained about 6.8 million people in the 16th century, and about 700,000 by 1992: see Grenand and Grenand (1993: 94). The Yana of Northern California had *c.* 1,900 members in 1846, but within 20 years of the arrival of white settlers, they were reduced to under 100: see Johnson (1978: 362).

[9] Annamalai (1998: 18). *Iatiku* 1.2 carried a report of a linguist who had taken an interest in the last two speakers of Gafat, Ethiopia, and was recording their language; but once they were away from their own environment, they caught a cold and died.

greater impact on communities and languages than anything else. UNAIDS, the joint UN programme on HIV/AIDS,[10] reports a world total of 33.4 million affected at the end of 1998, with 95% of all infections and deaths occurring in developing countries: 22.5 million in Sub-Saharan Africa, 6.7 million in South and South-east Asia, and 1.4 million in Latin America – areas which together contain over three-quarters of the world's languages. The rise of tuberculosis (which causes 30% of AIDS deaths) is a further factor. In the African countries worst affected – notably Botswana, Namibia, Swaziland, and Zimbabwe the disease has damaged a quarter of the population aged between 15 and 50. In these four countries, the effect on languages will be limited, because there are relatively few languages spoken (*c.* 80 in all). But in, say, Nigeria, where many of its 470 languages are spoken by tiny numbers, the effect of the epidemic, though so far causing fewer deaths (150,000 in 1997), is bound to be disproportionate.

The effects of famine and disease are intimately related to economic factors. There are now innumerable cases on record of the safety of a people being directly affected by the economic exploitation of their area by outsiders. *Desertification* is the name given to the environmental degradation of arid and semi-arid areas of the world through overcultivation, overgrazing, cash-cropping (which reduces the land available for producing food crops for the local people), deforestation, and bad irrigation practices, with changing climatic patterns (such as El Niño) also implicated.[11] Once the land loses its fertility, it

[10] *Aids Epidemic Update* (United Nations: UNAIDS), December 1998.
[11] *The Cambridge encyclopedia* (Crystal, 1997c), entry on 'desertification'.

is unable to support its population – a phenomenon which was repeatedly seen in Africa during the 1970s and 1980s, when desertification occurred throughout the Sahel. Unpredictable migrations take place, in which communities find it hard to preserve their integrity, and traditional cultural – and linguistic – dependencies are broken.

In parts of the world where indigenous natural resources have been subject to outside exploitation, the effect on the local people has been devastating, as is regularly documented by human rights organizations. The treatment of the communities of the Amazonian rain-forest continues to provide cause for international condemnation. Despite decades of effort to secure land rights for the indigenous peoples, and give them protection against the aggression of ranchers, miners, and loggers, reports of ethnic murder and displacement are still common. An extract from one report published by Amnesty International must suffice to represent what is a depressingly large file.[12] This one refers to a government decree which threatened the current demarcation of some 344 indigenous lands in Brazil:

Since the decree was passed, on 8 January 1996, several new invasions of indigenous lands have been reported. In the past unscrupulous local politicians and economic interests in many states, often backed by state authorities, have stimulated the invasion of indigenous lands by settlers, miners and loggers, playing on any uncertainty about the demarcation process. This has resulted in violent clashes and killings. The authorities at all levels have consistently failed to protect the fundamental

[12] Report by Linda Rabben for the Amnesty International News Service, 25 January 1996.

human rights of members of indigenous groups or bring those responsible for such attacks to justice.

Whilst Amnesty International takes no position on land disputes, the human rights organization has campaigned against human rights abuses suffered by Brazil's indigenous communities in recent years from those coveting their lands and the resources on them, who frequently act with official acquiescence or collusion. Amnesty International has repeatedly called on authorities at all levels to put an end to the almost universal impunity for killings, assaults, and threats to members of indigenous communities. Partial figures indicate that, during the last five years, at least 123 members of indigenous groups have been murdered by members of the non-indigenous population in land disputes. With few exceptions, no-one has been brought to justice for such killings. For example, to date no-one has been brought to trial for the massacre of 14 members of the Ticuna tribe in Amazonas in 1988, and for the massacre of 14 members of the Yanomami village of Haximu on the Brazil/Venezuelan border in 1993.

Rarely has the phrase 'for example' carried such unspoken resonance. In cases where a community has been displaced, many of the survivors, unwilling or unable to remain in their habitat, find their way to population centres, where they slowly lose their cultural identity within a milieu of poverty. To survive, they acquire as much as they can of a new language – in Brazil it would be Portuguese, or one of the creoles spoken in the region as lingua francas. The ethnic language tends not to outlast a generation – if the members of that generation survive at all.

In some parts of the world, it is the political, rather than the economic, situation in a country which is the immediate cause of the decimation or disappearance of a community. The damage may be the result of civil war, or of conflict on an international scale; for example, several Pacific and Indian Ocean island communities were caught up in the invasions and battles of the Second World War, with language endangerment one of the outcomes (e.g. in the Andaman Islands).[13] Long-standing ethnic or religious enmities may be implicated, as in parts of Africa. Bruce Connell's account of the decline of the Mambiloid cluster of languages (of which Kasabe was a member – see p. 1) provides an illustration:[14]

> The most commonly held belief is that the coming of the Fulani jihad during the 19th century, the subsequent enslavement of many and the massacring of resisters scattered and decimated their populations, to the point where their languages were no longer viable.

The circumstances may amount to genocide. Such claims have been made concerning the fate of the Nuba in Sudan and of the Ogoni in Nigeria.[15]

In many places, it is difficult to disentangle the political and economic factors. The disappearance of several languages in Colombia, for example, has been attributed to a mixture of aggressive circumstances.[16] One strand highlights a history of military conflict, in which several indigenous communities have been exterminated: some thirty languages are known to have become extinct since the arrival of the Spanish. Today, the conflict is more

---

[13] Annamalai (1998: 23). Another consequence of war is that archive records can be lost: in the case of Vanimo, in Papua New Guinea, all the vernacular language materials produced by missionaries over many years were destroyed during the fighting between the Japanese and Allied armies in the Second World War. See Landweer (1998: 65).
[14] Connell (1997: 27).   [15] Brenzinger (1998: 91).
[16] Seifart (1998: 8–10).

complex, involving regular, paramilitary, guerrilla, and criminal (drug-related) forces, operating in rural areas; members of ethnic communities find themselves embroiled in the conflicts, often suspected by one of these forces of acting as collaborators with the other(s). Another strand highlights the exploitation of small communities by organizations both from within the country and from outside, with reported instances of slave labour (for rubber production along the Amazon) and of forced migrations from rural areas to the cities. Whatever the balance of causes, the result has been the same – significant mortality of the people, and short-term community disintegration.[17]

Factors which change the people's culture

The people may live, but the language may still die. The second cluster of factors causing language loss has nothing directly to do with the physical safety of a people. The members of the community remain alive and well, often continuing to inhabit their traditional territory; but their language nonetheless goes into decline, and eventually

---

[17] For example, it is thought that the Andoke people were reduced from c. 10,000 in 1908 to c. 100 bilingual speakers in the 1970s, as a result of their enslavement for rubber exploitation: see Landaburu (1979). The Seifart article (fn. 16 above) actually expresses some optimism for the sixty or so indigenous languages still spoken in Colombia. A national organization now represents the people's interests at government level, and the 1991 Constitution for the first time gave the languages a level of recognition, making them official in their own territories, and guaranteeing bilingual education there. However, there is still a pressing need for linguistic analysis of many of the languages, and for appropriate teaching materials – work that is chiefly proceeding at the Colombian Centre for the Study of Indigenous Languages (*Centro Colombiano de Estudios de Lenguas Aborígines*). See, further, chapter 5.

disappears, to be replaced by some other language. The term most often encountered in this connection is *cultural assimilation*: one culture is influenced by a more dominant culture, and begins to lose its character as a result of its members adopting new behaviour and mores. This can happen in several ways. The dominance may be the result of demographic submersion – large numbers arrive in the community's territory, and swamp the indigenous people – as has happened repeatedly in the course of colonialism. Australia and North America are classic instances. Alternatively, one culture may exercise its dominance over another without a huge influx of immigration, perhaps through its initial military superiority or for economic reasons. Either way, language quickly becomes an emblem of that dominance, typically taking the form of a standard or official language associated with the incoming nation. Population size is not always critical: a smaller group can dominate a larger one – as was seen repeatedly in the European entry into Africa.

Nor is geographical proximity critical, for one culture to influence another. Especially during the twentieth century, circles of influence have become wider and wider and, in the case of the so-called Western consumer culture, now take in the whole globe. The factors are well known.[18] Urbanization has produced cities which act as magnets to rural communities, and developments in transport and communications have made it easier for country people to reach them. Within these cities they

---

[18] See Babe (1997), and other papers in Cliché (1997). The notion of 'extreme dynamism' as a characteristic of the age is the starting-point of Grenoble and Whaley (1998a: Preface).

have immediate access to the consumer society, with its specifically American biases, and the homogenization which contact of this kind inevitably brings. The learning of the dominant language – such as Spanish or Portuguese in South America, Swahili in much of East Africa, Quechua and Aymara in the Andean countries, and English virtually everywhere – immensely facilitates this process. Even if people stay in their rural setting, there is no escape (except for the most isolated communities), because the same transport systems which carry country people into the cities are used to convey consumer products and the associated advertising back to their communities. The centralization of power within the metropolis invariably results in an inevitable loss of autonomy for local communities, and often a sense of alienation as they realize that they are no longer in control of their own destinies, and that local needs are being disregarded by distant decision-makers. The language of the dominant culture infiltrates everywhere, reinforced by the relentless daily pressure of the media, and especially of television – an effect which Michael Krauss has likened to 'cultural nerve gas'.[19] Traditional knowledge and practices are quickly eroded. Herbert Schiller reinforces the point: referring to the way cultural homogenization is now threatening the entire globe, he comments, 'Everywhere local culture is facing submission from the mass-produced outpourings of commercial broadcasting', and in a later book makes the relevant reflection:[20]

---

[19] Krauss (1992: 6).
[20] First quotation from Schiller (1969: 113); second from Schiller (1976: 1); see also Babe (1997).

What does it matter if a national movement has struggled for years to achieve liberation if that condition, once gained, is undercut by values and aspirations derived from the apparently vanquished dominator?

When one culture assimilates to another, the sequence of events affecting the endangered language seem to be the same everywhere. There are three broad stages. The first is immense pressure on the people to speak the dominant language – pressure that can come from political, social, or economic sources. It might be 'top down', in the form of incentives, recommendations, or laws introduced by a government or national body; or it might be 'bottom up', in the form of fashionable trends or peer group pressures from within the society of which they form a part; or again, it might have no clear direction, emerging as the result of an interaction between sociopolitical and socioeconomic factors that are only partly recognized and understood. But wherever the pressure has come from, the result – stage two – is a period of emerging bilingualism, as people become increasingly efficient in their new language while still retaining competence in their old. Then, often quite quickly, this bilingualism starts to decline, with the old language giving way to the new. This leads to the third stage, in which the younger generation becomes increasingly proficient in the new language, identifying more with it, and finding their first language less relevant to their new needs. This is often accompanied by a feeling of shame about using the old language, on the part of the parents as well as their children. Parents use the old language less and less to their children, or in front of their children; and when more children come to be born within the new society, the adults find fewer opportunities to use that language to them. Those families which do continue to use the language find there are fewer other families to talk to, and their own usage becomes inward-looking and idiosyncratic, resulting in 'family dialects'. Outside the home, the children stop talking to each other in the language. Within a generation – sometimes even within a decade – a healthy bilingualism within a family can slip into a self-conscious semilingualism, and thence into a monolingualism which places that language one step nearer to extinction.[21]

Global forces being what they are, those concerned about the future of endangered languages know that it would be impossible nowadays to influence the factors which underlie the first stage in this process. And the third stage is, for most languages, too late. It is the second stage – the stage of emergent bilingualism – where there is a real chance to make progress. If the process of language decline is to be slowed down, stopped, or reversed, this (as we shall see in chapters 4 and 5) is where attention must be focused. Stephen Wurm sums it up in this way:

Many languages in danger of disappearing today would not be in this position today if it were not for the attitudes of most speakers of the large metropolitan languages with whom they are in contact, with most of those firmly believing that monolingualism is the normal and desirable state for people to be in and who, in consequence, put the speakers of such endangered languages before an either/or choice regarding their language: either to adopt their metropolitan language, or to remain

---

[21] Several commentators draw attention to the speed of this process: for example, England (1998: 102). For an example of the development of 'family dialects', see Furbee, Stanley, and Arkeketa (1998: 77).

outside the advantages stemming from its mastery in the culture in which their metropolitan language is dominant. These attitudes ... completely disregard the possibility of speakers of such endangered languages being bilingual in their own language and a given large metropolitan language, and as a result of cultural and social pressure from the monolingual metropolitan culture, this possibility rarely occurs to the speakers of the endangered minority languages.[22]

Why is this stage so important? It is because bilingualism offers a *modus vivendi* between the dominant and dominated language – an option for coexistence without confrontation. This is possible, in principle, because the reasons for the presence of the two languages are totally different. The dominant language is attractive because it facilitates outward movement from the indigenous community; there are new horizons which members of the community wish to reach towards, new standards of living to be achieved, a new quality of life to be pursued. (I do not consider it part of my brief, in this book, to reflect on whether this new life is better or worse than the old one.) The dominant language is necessary because it provides people with a bridge between the two worlds – an

---

[22] Wurm (1998: 193–4). The issue may also not occur to the speakers of the metropolitan language. As we have seen in chapter 2 (p. 59), monolingual people are not used to thinking about bilingualism as an asset, offering its speakers broader mental horizons, larger dimensions of knowledge, greater flexibility of thought, and greater understanding and tolerance of social differences. It simply is not part of their mindset. They are not against bilingualism, as such; rather, by being part of a long colonialist tradition, monolingualism has come to be the natural way of life. Few of the people in my own social milieu to whom I have introduced the notion of bilingualism as a benefit or a solution are against the idea: it just had not occurred to them.

intelligibility bridge, without which their progress would be negligible. The dominated language, by contrast, has quite another role. By definition, it has no value as an international or intercultural lingua franca; it cannot facilitate communication between peoples; it is not outward-looking. It is there for the opposite reason: to express the identity of the speakers as members of their community. It is inward-looking – but in the best sense (see chapter 2) – fostering family ties, maintaining social relationships, preserving historical links, giving people a sense of their 'pedigree' (p. 54). The dominant language cannot do this:[23] it has its own identity; those who speak it as a mother tongue have their own pedigree. Only the dominated language can refresh the identity of an indigenous community – the part that other languages cannot reach.

But for this to happen, the terminology of 'domination' must disappear. Healthy bilingualism is a state in which two languages are seen as complementary, not in competition – fulfilling different roles, with each language being seen in a rewarding light.[24] Labels such as 'dominated' hardly help foster the positive attitudes which are needed; and, when it comes to endangered languages, attitude is what counts – how people look at their language, and what they

---

[23] Only at the point where people have completely lost their sense of identification with their ethnic origins will the new language offer an alternative and comfortable linguistic home (at which point, the cultural assimilation would be complete).

[24] Multilingualism was described as mankind's natural state, in chapter 2. For a comprehensive debunking of the myths associated with bilingualism, and an encyclopedic guide to its strengths, see the references in ch. 2, fn. 45.

feel about it when they do. If speakers take pride in their language, enjoy listening to others using it well, use it themselves whenever they can and as creatively as they can, and provide occasions when the language can be heard, the conditions are favourable for maintenance. Stage 2, in such a setting, is likely to last a long time. Conversely, if people are embarrassed to use their language, switch into the dominant language whenever they can, tell jokes where the speaker of the endangered language is the butt, and avoid occasions where the language is celebrated, then stage 2 is likely to last for only a short time. Fostering positive language attitudes is, accordingly, one of the most important initiatives to be achieved in the task of language preservation (see, further, chapter 4).

Languages decline when these positive attitudes are missing. And in so many cases they *are* missing. The climate is against them, often for political reasons. For example, most of the governments of Africa would see linguistic diversity as a threat to national unity – to the task of building a nation.[25] Minorities are a source of concern to these governments because of the well-attested history of ethnic conflict throughout the region. The members of the government in power themselves often belong to a particular ethnic group. Proposals to strengthen ethnic status or loyalty can thus be treated with suspicion; and because language is so closely bound up with ethnic identity, proposals to strengthen minority languages can be especially suspect. Indeed, it is quite possible for an indigenous community to be put in danger simply by

---

[25] But not, notably, Eritrea, which has gone so far as to refuse to assign official status to any of its languages.

allowing outsiders in to record their language.[26] The authorities tend to be nervous – and perhaps with cause, for sociopolitical outcomes are never predictable, and there are many known cases of languages being used as tools of resistance against oppressive regimes, or as a means of communicating information secretly in wartime.[27] The powerful role of language as a way of fomenting revolution was recognized by the first slave traders, who deliberately mixed people with different language backgrounds in the ships bound for America, so that they could not communicate effectively with each other. A similar initiative led to Indian tribes with different language backgrounds being placed together on reservations in North America, so that they were forced to learn English.[28] And myths still abound: in one report, a Colombian army officer described the Embera, a Pacific coastal people, as simply having made up their language in order to confuse white people.[29]

Open antipathy is not found everywhere. In South America, for example, indigenous languages are not

---

[26] Brenzinger (1998: 89).
[27] A little-known fact is that American Indian languages have been used in this way: during both World Wars, members of at least seventeen tribes served as 'code talkers' for US forces in Europe and the Pacific, including a large number of Navajo who worked with US Marines in the Second World War: see Paul (1973), Bixler (1992). In 1999 a campaign was underway to have the US government recognize their special service through the award of Medals of Honor.
[28] Kinkade (1991: 157).
[29] Seifart (1998: 9). Note also this comment in a newspaper report on the situation of some of the Khoisan peoples of Southern Africa (Koch and Maslamoney, 1997): 'Farmers and employers threaten people who use Khoekhoegowap [Nam] because, in a paranoia that is common to all oppressors, they believe the speakers are plotting subversion.'

usually considered a threat to national unity, presumably because the states have had much longer to become established. The attitude there is more one of indifference than antagonism.[30] The antipathy may also take more subtle forms. People find they have fewer opportunities to use their language, because it has been officially marginalized. It is not found in official domains, such as the local offices of the civil service and the local banks. It is not found in the media. It is not found as the language of higher education: for example, none of the 1,200 or so languages indigenous to Africa is currently used as a medium of instruction in secondary schools there.[31] The language gradually disappears from the 'serious' side of life, with religion usually the last domain to be affected. Its presence may still be strong in some domains, such as the arts, popular entertainment, and folklore, but these are perceived to be domains with less status. From a political point of view, the language is becoming invisible. American sociolinguist Joshua Fishman once referred to this state of affairs as the 'folklorization' of a language – the use of an indigenous language only in irrelevant or unimportant domains.[32] And with each loss of a domain, it

[30] Adelaar (1998: 9). Indifference, of course, is no help, because if nothing is being done to counter a declining trend, the situation will simply deteriorate. Less obviously, even political support for an endangered language might not change public attitudes, if experience has fostered in local people the view that the government is not to be trusted or that its motives are suspect.

[31] Brenzinger (1998: 95).

[32] Fishman (1987). Others have talked about languages being 'deprived' of domains: see Bamgbose (1997). The way languages can become invisible is illustrated for India by Annamalai (1998: 20ff., 30), who also refers to the way a language's status can be altered as an effect of census taking. The identity of a language is immediately obscured, as a political

should be noted, there is a loss of vocabulary, discourse patterns, and stylistic range. It is easy to see how a language could eventually die, simply because, having been denuded of most of its domains, there is hardly any subject-matter left for people to talk about, and hardly any vocabulary left to do it with. It becomes a form of behaviour familiar only to the enthusiast, the specialist, and the seeker after curiosities. It lacks prestige.

This is the chief reason why even those languages with very large numbers of speakers may not be safe, in the long run: their status may be gradually eroded until no one wants to use them. In South America, Quechua and Aymara, in all their varieties, currently have well over a million speakers each; but urban migration to the coastal cities of Peru is significantly reducing the figure, with people shifting to Spanish.[33] This would not be so serious if the language was being strongly maintained in rural areas; but attitudes are reported to be changing there. The indigenous languages are being viewed *by their speakers* as a sign of backwardness, or as a hindrance to making improvements in social standing. They have no confidence in them. The negative attitudes may be so entrenched that even when the authorities get around to doing something about it – introducing community projects, protective measures, or official language policies – the indigenous community may greet their efforts with unenthusiasm, scepticism, or outright hostility.

reality, if its speakers are lumped together with others under some general census heading, or included as a 'variety' of a more dominant language.

[33] Adelaar (1998: 6).

But people have to get their negative attitudes from somewhere. One isn't born with feelings of shame and a lack of self-confidence about one's language. Where do they come from? In virtually all cases, they are introduced by a more dominant culture, whose members stigmatize the people in such terms as stupid, lazy, and barbaric (often, despite the evidence of great artistic achievements in the people's past, as in the case of the Mayas and Aztecs), and their language as ignorant, backward, deformed, inadequate, or even (in the case of some missionaries) a creation of the devil. Akira Yamomoto quotes a typical statement, made by a nineteenth-century commissioner of Indian affairs in the USA: 'The instruction of the Indians in the vernacular is not only of no use to them, but is detrimental to the cause of their education and civilization.'[34] These attitudes are then reinforced through the introduction of practices which penalize the use of the local language. Kenyan author Ngugi wa Thiong'o recalled such experiences from his schooldays, when English was the educational norm:[35]

one of the most humiliating experiences was to be caught speaking Gikuyu in the vicinity of the school. The culprit was given corporal punishment – three to five strokes of the cane on the bare buttocks – or was made to carry a metal plate around the neck with inscriptions such as I AM STUPID or I AM A DONKEY. Sometimes the culprits were fined money they could hardly afford. And how did the teachers catch the culprits? A button was initially given to one pupil who was supposed to hand it over to whoever was caught speaking his mother tongue. Whoever had the button at the end of the day

[34] Yamamoto (1998a: 215).   [35] Ngugi wa Thiong'o (1986: 11).

would sing who had given it to him and the ensuing process would bring out all the culprits of the day. Thus children were turned into witch-hunters and in the process were being taught the lucrative value of being a traitor to one's immediate community.

Similar experiences have been reported from many parts of the world, and not only in relation to English; for example, French, Spanish, and Portuguese policies of suppression were common in Africa and Latin America; the Japanese suppressed Ainu in Japan. Indigenous languages would be prohibited in missions and boarding schools. Wales had the Welsh Not, known especially in the nineteenth century. This was a piece of wood or slate with the letters 'WN' cut into it, hung round the neck of a pupil caught speaking Welsh; it would be passed on to another heard using the language, and the one wearing it at the end of the day would be punished. Ireland had a similar practice. In other places, washing the mouth out with soap was popular: as a Tlingit man from Alaska put it – 'Whenever I speak Tlingit, I can still taste the soap.'[36] But whatever the mechanism, the result was the same: a growing sense of inferiority or shame about one's language, a reluctance or embarrassment to use the language for fear of evoking further condemnation, and a natural desire to avoid having one's children exposed to the same experience. If people believe, rightly or wrongly, that it is their ancestral language which has kept them down, or

[36] The Tlingit example is from Dauenhauer and Dauenhauer (1998: 65). This also contains a useful discussion of the factors underlying negative attitudes in indigenous language use. See also, for North America, Mithun (1998: 182). For Ainu, see Sawai (1998: 183).

that they were held back from social advancement by an inability to speak the dominant language well, it is not surprising to find them antipathetic towards preservation, and unsupportive when language maintenance projects are in place (such as in schools). And when this view is reinforced by the opinions of the young people them- selves – who may also see the old language as irrelevant or a hindrance, and think of the older people who do still speak it as backward or ignorant – it is only to be expected that negative attitudes pervade the whole of a community.[37]

The deliberate attempt by speakers of one language to crush those of another has often been attested, and when there is evidence that this has taken place, such as at various points in colonial history, some authors have felt the need to use suitably dramatic language, talking about 'language murder' or 'linguicide'. The way antagonism can be focused on a language has been powerfully cap- tured by Harold Pinter, in his play *Mountain language* (1988, Act I), where at one point an officer addresses a group of women in this way:

Now hear this. You are mountain people. You hear me? Your language is dead. It is forbidden. It is not permitted to speak your mountain language in this place. You cannot speak your language to your men. It is not permitted. Do you understand?

---

[37] It should also be mentioned that negative attitudes are easily reinforced through repeated casual reference to a language's endangered state, especially when the remarks are made by outsiders. It is difficult to instil enthusiasm for preservation among community members if they are continually being told that their language is 'dying' or even already 'dead'. According to Sawai (1998: 185), this was a factor in the decline of Ainu.

You may not speak it. It is outlawed. You may speak only the language of the capital. That is the only language permitted in this place. You will be badly punished if you attempt to speak your mountain language in this place. This is a military decree. It is the law. Your language is forbidden. It is dead. No one is allowed to speak your language. Your language no longer exists.

Those are indeed the tones of language murder. However, the point has also been made that this terminology is not always appropriate: faced with a situation where people make a conscious decision to stop using their language, or not to pass it on to their children, seeing it as an intolerable burden, a better description might be 'language suicide'. This certainly seems to be more often the case in settings where English is the desirable goal – which is one reason why talk of English as a 'killer language' is a gross oversimplification of a complex situation.[38] The effects of a dominant language vary markedly in different parts of the world, as do attitudes towards it. In Australia, the presence of English has, directly or indirectly, caused great linguistic devastation, with 90% of languages moribund. But English is not the language which is dominant throughout Latin America: if languages are dying there, it is not through any 'fault' of English. Moreover, the presence of a dominant language does not automatically result in a 90% extinction rate.

---

[38] For a sensible discussion of terms such as 'murder', 'persecution', and 'suicide' in relation to language, see Edwards (1985: 51–3). While there are some cases where the terms are metaphorically appropriate, his conclusion should be noted: 'Discussions of language decline and death would do well to avoid terms like "murder" and "suicide" altogether, and to emphasise the complexities of social situations in which these phenomena occur.'

Russian has long been dominant in the countries of the former USSR, but there the destruction of local languages has been estimated to be only (sic) 50%.[39]

Another aspect of the complexity is the way in which the preservation of an endangered language may actually be aided by the growing presence of the dominant language within a region, in that it forces the speakers to confront the situation in which they find themselves, and may generate greater levels of support for revitalization than would otherwise be the case. A classic case is the dramatic support given to Welsh, which led to the formation of the Welsh Language Society (Cymdeithas yr Iaith Gymraeg) in 1962, and a number of activist measures, most famously in 1980, when the commencement of a fast to the death by Gwynfor Evans, leader of the Welsh nationalist party, Plaid Cymru, forced the government to honour election pledges on a Welsh television channel.[40] And in South America, the 1992 quincentennial commemoration of the arrival of the Spanish prompted a wide range of activities in support of indigenous rights.[41]

When another language is perceived to be so desirable and useful, it is hardly surprising that people want to learn it; and if it helps them get on in life, this is obviously a good thing. The argument is not that people should not learn a metropolitan language. The argument is that there is no necessary confrontation between this new language and the old. The pride which everyone feels when they succeed in acquiring a new language should not make them any less proud of the language they already have.

[39] Krauss (1992: 5).   [40] For a historical review, see Bellin (1984).
[41] Grinevald (1998: 142).

If a bilingual ethos were more manifest in the metropolitan community, then there would be far less voluntary abandonment of language by indigenous speakers, and the terminology of threat would not be as widespread as it currently is.[42]

Conclusion

Many factors contribute to the phenomenon of language death, so the diagnosis of pathological situations is always going to be complex. Sociolinguists have tried to identify a single major factor to explain the way people shift from one language to another, but all such attempts have been controversial. For example, one proposal identifies the need for people to acquire the dominant language in order to get a good job (or to ensure that their children get a good job): it is a plausible hypothesis in many areas (it certainly explains the kind of case illustrated by my Johannesburg anecdote, p. 18), but it may be less relevant in others, where the type of educational system, the presence of the media, or the nature of political pressures can be more important considerations. Languages are not like people, in this respect: it is not usually possible to write a single cause on the death certificate for a language.

Because there are so many factors involved, a language does not usually die out uniformly. It might be

---

[42] In the absence of this ethos, in most developed countries, there is the irony that the more languages you have, the more likely you are low down in the social hierarchy. Hale (1995: 5) is among those who has observed this, in his work with the Ulwa of Nicaragua: the Twahka people, at the bottom of the social order, need five languages in order to get by.

disappearing in one location but not (yet) in others, for a range of different reasons. Some countries have created locations for cultural conservation – such as reservations or protected areas – where a language might be quite healthy, though rapidly dying out elsewhere. Sometimes, the variation in vitality has come about through variations in the history of natural settlement: in Colombia, the people of the mountains preserve their languages better than those of the lowlands and rainforests; in Ireland, the western seaboard region known as the Gaeltacht has a stronger concentration of Irish than elsewhere.[43] Catastrophic events aside, language death is a gradual and varied process, with the general trends affecting different members or sections of a community in different ways. This is one of the reasons why a community usually does not realize that its language is in danger until too late.

Some of the factors which we have reviewed above are uncontroversially final, in their causative role: there is no arguing with a tsunami. But with the range of cultural factors, it is possible to see several outcomes, depending on the nature of a country's history and circumstances, its language policies (if it has any), and the extent to which planning strategies are being resourced and implemented. A significant demographic growth within an indigenous community can make more people available to use a language (though this factor becomes otiose if parental attitudes are antipathetic). There will be a more positive outcome if the community has a strong sense of cultural

---

[43] For Colombia, see Seifart (1998); for Ireland, see John Edwards (1985: 53ff.); for the similar situation in the Scottish Gaeltacht, see Watson (1991: 41–59).

or religious identity, endogamous marriage practices, or a vibrant crafts or literary tradition. The community's ability to make its presence felt in the local media can be important – it was a major factor in the reversal of the decline of Welsh, for example. The bringing in of outsiders can be a help or a hindrance, depending on the extent to which their presence is viewed as a (religious, cultural, political) threat. And the remoteness of the community from other groups is a critical issue. Indeed, some say that the only way for a small language to survive is for its speakers to remain in isolation – a rare option, nowadays.

The forces which cause language death are so massive that it is difficult to see how any of them could be reversed. The prospect in a few hundred years of just one language per nation, and then just one language for the whole world, which several scholars have asserted, is indeed real.[44] It is likely that there will be some degree of renewal of the language stock, of course, through the development of new languages: as we have seen in chapter 1 (pp. 11–12), some of the new varieties of English may, in the course of time, become sufficiently distinct to be justifiably called separate languages (Scots, Ebonics, Australian Aboriginal English, Singlish, etc.). The forces which are currently making Serbian, Croatian, and Bosnian increasingly different from each other could one day – though it is a long way off – produce three mutually unintelligible languages. And new pidgins and creoles are always emerging. But there are not many examples like this. As Michael Krauss has put it: 'We cannot look forward to rediversification to compensate to any significant degree for the loss.'[45] But he adds: 'However, the degree of that loss can be affected by our response to the threat. The difference between the best and worst scenarios, say loss of half [the world's languages] and loss of 95%, is still very great.' Indeed it is. And it is the growing realization that a response to the threat is possible which has motivated the enormous range of activities reported in chapters 4 and 5.

---

[45] Krauss (1998: 106).

4

Where do we begin?

~

Faced with a problem of such worldwide scale, and such a limited time frame in many instances, the need for cool, careful, and coordinated action is evident. There are now enough case studies of revitalization from around the world to show that language loss is not always inevitable. A great deal can be done – and already has been done – by indigenous communities, local support groups, and outside bodies. Professional linguistic concern grew significantly during the 1990s, as has been noted in the Preface. International awareness of language rights also took a significant step forward in that decade, notably with the formulation of the Barcelona Universal Declaration of Linguistic Rights.[1] At the same time, the increased attention has resulted in the true complexities of the situation beginning to be unravelled. The notion of language maintenance is rarely as straightforward as it seems. Even the relatively transparent task of making a linguistic recording of an endangered language turns out to have many hidden

[1] A document prepared over a two-year period, promoted by the International PEN Club's Translations and Linguistic Rights Committee and the Escarré International Centre for Ethnic Minorities and Nations, with the moral and technical support of UNESCO, and published following an international conference in 1996, at which nearly ninety states were represented. Discussion about its content was still ongoing at the time of writing, as work continued towards the goal of making it an International Convention of the United Nations. See Appendix for contact details.

pitfalls. We therefore need to review the situation as a whole, without minimizing the difficulties. As one research team has remarked:[2]

> The paradoxical situation is that the languages will certainly die unless we do something; but, the reality is that they may also die even if we do something. Therefore, what do we do?

The remainder of this book tries to answer that question. So where do we begin?

Establishing the top priorities

The top priority, it would appear, is information gathering. Although there may be 3,000 or more languages at risk, it is plain from the earlier chapters that they are not all in the same state of endangerment. Some are in their final stages now; some have a great deal of life left in them. Given that time, personnel, and resources are limited, it is crucial to establish what the really urgent cases are. That was the chief motivation for the growth, during the 1990s, of the various organizations concerned with endangered languages (see Appendix), and in particular – as its name suggests – of the International Clearing House for Endangered Languages in Tokyo. Fact-finding and prioritization are the immediate needs. A typical statement from one of the national organizations makes the same point: 'the first step in language rescue must be an informative assessment of a language's current situation'.[3] And the editors of a recent collection of essays concur: 'Only with detailed and comprehensive data on

---

[2] Dauenhauer and Dauenhauer (1998: 78).   [3] Ostler (1997: 5).

language vitality is long-term prediction of the global linguistic picture a real possibility.'[4]

But information gathering does not exist in a vacuum. What kind of information is to be gathered? As we have seen in chapter 3, facts about the numbers of speakers are only one of the things we need to know. Just as important are facts about the context in which the speakers live, and facts about the attitudes displayed – both by the speakers themselves and by the larger community of which they are a part. The relevant interest is in linguistic vitality, and the possibility of revitalization, so assessments need to take into account facts about speaker fluency, accuracy, and age levels in order to arrive at a proper evaluation of the likelihood of continuity. Indeed, just how many different kinds of relevant facts are there? What is the difference between an 'informative' and an 'uninforma-tive' assessment? Plainly, we also need a theoretical framework to orientate the fact-finding, and to provide guidelines about assessment and diagnosis. Such a frame-work would yield models which could identify and inter-relate the relevant variables involved in endangerment, and these models would generate empirical hypotheses about such matters as rate of decline or stages in revival. It is already evident that there can be no such thing as a unified intervention procedure, given that there are so many kinds of endangerment, and so many possible ways of helping. Different communities, as we have seen, have different kinds of attitudes and aspirations in relation to their language. A typological statement may be all that is

---

[4] Grenoble and Whaley (1998a: viii). For an example of a detailed questionnaire approach to fact-finding, see Mikhalchenko (1998).

achievable in the immediate future, therefore, identifying the similarities and differences between endangered situations; but even to reach that point, we need a theoretical framework which has achieved some degree of consensus. It is no good postponing this step until 'we have all the facts'. We shall never have all the facts.

As I write, no such framework exists. Studies of endangered languages are at a stage where they use widely different frames of reference and terminology. Even the subject as a whole has no agreed name.[5] Terms such as *obsolescent*, *moribund*, and *endangered* are employed in a variety of senses. The people affected are described differently (e.g. *terminal speakers*, *semi-speakers*). The widely encountered metaphor of *critical mass* (of speakers needed to maintain a language) has not been operationalized. Lists of causative factors (such as the one I compiled myself in chapter 3) are eclectic and impressionistic, well motivated by individual case studies, but lacking in generality. Enough studies have now been carried out, from a sufficiently wide range of places, for the scale of the problem to be appreciated. A great deal of perceptive analysis has taken place, and the urgency of the need has prompted many *ad hoc* proposals about ways of improving individual endangered situations. But without a general framework, the opportunities for cross-fertilization of thought are limited. At grass-roots level, there must be an enormous amount of 'rediscovering the wheel' going on around the world, as researchers and community advisers, uncertain whether other initiatives and experiences apply

---

[5] *Perilinguistics* was proposed by Matisoff (1991: 201, 224). Personally, I prefer the more dynamic resonance of *preventive linguistics* (cf. p. 149).

to them, promote activities of their own devising. In a climate of urgency, at times almost of panic, it is understandable to see a philosophy of 'anything is better than nothing' so widespread. But we know from other fields, such as speech therapy and foreign language teaching, that a policy of 'diving in', or of reacting only to the most apparent needs, can produce results that are short-term and inefficient. In a field where time is of the essence, and money very short, the need to keep some level of theoretical enquiry operating alongside the pressing demands of empirical work is therefore essential. This is also a top priority.

Some progress has been made since Einar Haugen's largely ignored call for a 'typology of ecological classification', which would 'tell us something about where the language stands and where it is going in comparison with the other languages of the world',[6] but most of the work has been in relation to languages in general, or to minority languages, regardless of whether they are endangered or not. It is possible, of course, to adapt proposals in this direction, and some efforts have been made to do this. For example, a typological framework devised by John Edwards for minority languages recognizes eleven relevant factors, each of which is applied to *languages*, their *speakers*, and the *settings* in which they speak: demographic, sociological, linguistic, psychological, historical, political, geographical, educational, religious, economic, and technological.[7] Lenore Grenoble and Lindsay

---

[6] Haugen (1971: 25). This title was given to his collection of essays, *The ecology of language* (Haugen, 1972). See also p. 42 above.

[7] Edwards (1992).

Whaley, focusing on endangered languages, suggest literacy as an additional factor, and propose a hierarchical organization of all factors, giving the economically based variables priority. They also extend the model to include various levels of external influence upon a language – local, regional, national, and extra-national.[8] This is exactly how a typological framework develops, through a process of intellectual reflection in the light of case studies. Certain factors, notably economic power, social status, and density of speakers, are going to rank highly in most situations. But establishing priorities takes time. Moreover, some of the issues are notoriously difficult to explore, such as assessing a person's level of comprehension ability, or determining a speaker's proficiency in controlling the range of stylistic features in a language.

Fact-finding and the development of a theoretical perspective should be two sides of the same coin. But for either to proceed, there have to be coins. What the coins do is pay for the job to be done. It is important, therefore, to have a sense of the costs involved – or at least of their order of magnitude. As far as a first encounter with a language is concerned, a thumbnail calculation provided by the Foundation for Endangered Languages[9] suggested that £35,000 (c. $56,000) per language would provide a basic (A-level) grammar and dictionary, assuming two years of work by one linguist. Dixon estimates that, to do a good job, we need to allow a linguist three years, and there would then not be much change from $200,000 (c. £125,000) after taking into account a salary, fees for

---

[8] Grenoble and Whaley (1998b).   [9] Editorial, in *Iatiku* 1.1.

indigenous language consultants, travel, equipment, accommodation, publication of the findings, and the provision of basic facilities for revitalization.[10] Gerdts takes an even broader view, anticipating in-depth studies, the development of an audio-visual archive, and a wider range of publications and teaching materials: she concludes that the estimate per language would be more like fifteen years and $2 million (*c.* £1.25 million).[11] Conditions vary so much that it is difficult to generalize, but a figure of £40,000 (*c.* $64,000) a year per language cannot be far from the truth. If we devoted that amount of effort over three years for each of the 3,000 cases referred to in chapter 1, we would be talking about some £360 million ($575 million). That may seem like a lot of money; but, to put it in perspective, it is equivalent to just over one day's OPEC oil revenues (in an average year).

Fund-raising, whether carried out at international, national, regional, or local levels, is therefore another top priority. And funds do not come unless people are aware of the urgency of a need and convinced of its desirability (see chapter 2). Fostering a climate of opinion thus has to be carried on in parallel with the above two activities, which means a wide range of public relations and political initiatives. Endangered languages have to be given a higher profile with the public, which means making maximum use of the media, and devising appropriate publicity campaigns. Although many areas of world concern have attracted public support by being assigned official 'days', 'weeks', 'months', and 'years' – for example, 1997 was the international year of the coral reef, 1998 the

---

[10] Dixon (1997: 138).   [11] Gerdts (1998: 14).

international year of the ocean – lost, endangered, or dying languages have not been given such attention.[12]

Perhaps the lack of awareness of endangered languages is simply another manifestation of the general lack of awareness about language among the public at large. Certainly, this is not the first time that language professionals have bemoaned the apparent absence of public interest in their field, complaining about poor levels of investment or resources, or pointing to the relatively low salaries found in linguistic specialisms. Speech and language therapy (or pathology) is one such field, where very similar arguments to those currently being reviewed in relation to language endangerment have been loudly and repeatedly made since the 1970s.[13] It is perhaps the climate of the time. All language professionals have suffered the consequences of a general malaise about language study which has long been present among the general public – an inevitable consequence (in my view) of two centuries of language teaching in which prescriptivism and purism produced a mentality suspicious of diversity, variation, and change, and a terminology whose Latinate origins crushed the spontaneous interest in language of most of those who came into contact with it.[14] Not that

---

[12] The European Bureau of Lesser Used Languages did however organize the first European Language Day, on 12 April 1997.

[13] See, for example, some of the arguments in Crystal (1982).

[14] Two specific examples of the consequences, from my own experience. I once had the opportunity to ask the purchasing manager of a major UK national book-chain why none of a paperback series on linguistics was available on its shelves, and was told that language was too difficult for the average purchaser; when I asked him what he meant, he talked about his bad memories of traditional grammar in school. I have also encountered the same response on several occasions (from different

the task of teaching about language is easy. On the contrary: it has always proved extremely difficult to convey the facts about language to the public, language being by its nature so abstract and complex. But there have been enough successful cases of language presentation through books and broadcasting to demonstrate that the task can be done; and when it *is* done, a warmly interested response is widespread – for most people do have an intuitive curiosity about language matters (at least, in their own language), whether it be the history of words, the character of local accents and dialects, or the origins of personal names and place names. Fortunately, there are clear signs that the climate is now changing, in the form of new language curricula in several parts of the world; the excitement and fascination of language study has been well captured by new generations of teachers.[15] But of course there is an inevitable time lag before the students who will benefit from this teaching reach sufficiently influential positions in society for their views to make a difference. As a consequence, the promotion of a fresh public attitude towards language in general (and towards endangered languages in particular) remains a current priority.

Several linguists engaged in this work have seen the need to become engaged with politicians and public bodies, and to get them thinking about language policies and practices. One puts it this way:[16]

broadcasting companies) when trying to establish why there has never been a blockbuster series on linguistics on either radio or television.
[15] See the discussions in Brumfit (1995), Sealey (1996), Crystal (1999).
[16] Rhydwen (1998: 104).

There are many ways to work towards slowing the erosion of linguistic diversity and one task is to develop and diversify ways that this might happen, to engage with people who are not professional linguists and to be open to innovative ways of thinking and acting.

The problem varies among countries. In former colonialist nations, in particular, linguists have to cope with a general inexperience of bilingualism, which makes it more difficult than it should be to get the message across. The greater the amount of foreign language learning in a country, whether in the home or in school, the easier this aspect of the task becomes. The chief aim is to develop in people a sense of the value of a language, and of what is lost when a language dies – the kind of arguments reviewed in chapter 2. There is an urgent need for memorable ways of talking, to capture what is involved: we have to develop ear-catching metaphors – language as a 'national treasure', perhaps, or as a 'cause for celebration', or a 'natural resource'. The two-way relationship with ecology needs to be developed: not only does an ecological frame of reference enter into language discussion; language issues need to become part of general ecological thinking.[17] Conferences and campaigns about the environment need

[17] The first joint meeting on the loss of cultural and biological diversity, with a focus on language, took place at the University of California, Berkeley, in 1996: 'Endangered Languages, Endangered Knowledge, Endangered Environments'. See the report in *Iatiku* 4. 14–16. The call for an ecological perspective for language goes back a generation, at least to Haugen's unjustly neglected paper (1971: 19): 'Language ecology may be defined as the study of interactions between any given language and its environment ... Language exists only in the minds of its users, and it only functions in relating these users to one another and to nature, i.e. their social and natural environment.'

to include language as part of their remit. A general concern about conservation is already out there, as has been seen in the many national ecological campaigns about climate, biology, and heritage; it now needs to be focused on language. This was the chief motivation leading to the establishment of one of the new pressure groups of the 1990s, Terralingua (see Appendix), one of whose goals is:

To illuminate the connections between cultural and biological diversity by establishing working relationships with scientific/ professional organizations and individuals who are interested in preserving cultural diversity (such as linguists, educators, anthropologists, ethnologists, cultural workers, native advocates, cultural geographers, sociologists, and so on) and those who are interested in preserving biological diversity (such as biologists, botanists, ecologists, zoologists, physical geographers, ethnobiologists, ethnoecologists, conservationists, environmental advocates, natural resource managers, and so on), thus promoting the joint preservation and perpetuation of cultural and biological diversity.

In countries where a language focus is already present, such as in Wales or Quebec, where linguistic issues are daily news, there is still a need for action. Awareness and concern have to be fostered about the problem as it exists worldwide, because all minority and endangered languages will benefit from a universal consciousness-raising about linguistic diversity. Language supporters everywhere are on the same side – but they need to realize this, and devise ways of showing it and capitalizing on it.[18] Although there

---

[18] This may in fact be an unrealistic expectation. Quite naturally, an indigenous community is preoccupied with its own situation, and unlikely to be much interested in endangered-language situations

are now organizations for professionals to keep in touch with each other, only limited progress has yet been made in providing mechanisms to foster international collaboration at grass-roots level. Some parts of the world have come to be relatively well served: Europe, for example, has the European Bureau of Lesser Used Languages, established in 1982, with its regular information bulletin, *Contact* (see Appendix). There have also been occasional publications in which people from different nations tell each other about the language situation in their own country,[19] and there is a growing use being made of the Internet for this purpose. But on the whole, apart from a minority of politicians, language activists, and professional linguists, people in one part of the world are largely unaware of what is going on in other places. The need for a global perspective on language endangerment is therefore urgent, and its importance cannot be overestimated. It is not simply a question of people learning from each other's situations and solutions. People need inspiration and encouragement – especially when confronting recalcitrant governments; and awareness that they are not alone, and that there are channels which can be used to elicit international co-operation, can make a lot of difference.

Within a country, people do not change their minds, or develop positive attitudes about endangered languages, just by being given information; the arguments need to capture their emotions. In particular, art forms need to be

---

elsewhere in the world. The levels of mutual interest and activism achieved in Europe, Australia, and the USA in recent years are not typical of most places, and even there they tend to have a regional focus.
[19] Iorwerth (1995).

brought to bear on the issue. There are still far too few poems, plays, novels, and other genres in which the notion of language is the theme.[20] Nor should music, painting, sculpture, dance, and other forms of artistic expression be left out of consideration. To take just one example from one place in one year: a piece of sculpture in New York in 1997–8.[21] There is a report, probably apocryphal, of an event which took place when the explorer Alexander von Humboldt was searching for the source of the Orinoco, in South America, in 1801. He met some Carib Indians who had recently exterminated a neighbouring tribe (possibly a Maypure group) and captured some of their domesticated parrots. The parrots still spoke words of the now extinct language, and von Humboldt – so the story goes – was able to transcribe some of them. Having heard this story, Rachel Berwick, professor of sculpture at Yale University, saw its intriguing possibilities, and constructed an artwork based upon it: she designed a special enclosure in which were displayed two Amazon parrots who had been trained to speak some words from Maypure, and this was then exhibited at various venues in 1997–8. By all accounts, the venture focused the mind wonderfully. So, if sculpture, why not – music? Is there yet a symphony for dying languages? Has there been a pop concert in support of Language Aid? It would be good to see some of these initiatives in the opening decades of the new millennium.

---

[20] Examples include Harold Pinter's play, *Mountain language* (1988); Margaret Atwood's poem, 'Marsh languages', in *Morning in the burned house* (1995); David Malouf's short story, 'The only speaker of his tongue' (1985); and my own play, *Living on* (1998).

[21] Reviewed in Holt (1998).

Bottom-up initiatives are a top priority too, for they help to form the ground swell of public opinion which can make governments act. A considerable amount of top-down action has already taken place, at least in those regions where minority-language supporters have been most active. But in many parts of the world, vociferous activism on behalf of minority languages is absent or suppressed. Governments may be indifferent or antagonistic (see chapter 3). Statistics about speakers can be manipulated or distorted. And even in the most active regions, the concept of endangerment is often not given the attention it should be.[22] In Europe, the focus has tended to be more on language rights than on endangerment. Also, there is still some way to go before declarations concerning language issues are given global status. In the meantime, the need for political lobbying and effective agitation remains strong.

The notion of 'top-down' applies not only at international level but also within individual countries and in localized regions. The development of appropriate structures at national level is a priority, especially in parts of the world which have large numbers of indigenous languages and no real history of study or concern. One of the most promising signs during the last few years, in fact, has been the establishment of new academic centres within a number of countries, demonstrating by their existence a fresh sense of language values; examples

---

[22] In 1999, for example, I found myself in correspondence with the British Foreign Office over a foreign affairs committee report on the implementation of a policy document on human rights which referred to every conceivable category of right – except language.

include the Colombian Centre for Study of Indigenous Languages at Bogotá, the Museu Paraense Emilio Goeldi at Belém, Brazil, the Academy of Mayan Languages in Guatemala, the Hokkaido Ainu Culture Research Center in Sapporo, and the Center for Endangered Languages at Jos, Nigeria. These centres carry out several roles simultaneously: in addition to fact-finding and language description, they provide a channel of communication between local community and government, and a mechanism for directing energies, funds, and revitalization activities. They give indigenous languages an institutionalized presence, and thus prestige; for without prestige, and the power which this brings, no language movement can succeed. Some of the difficulties which such centres encounter will be reviewed below.

Several priorities have been identified in this section, and it seems impossible to choose between them. Nor should it be necessary to choose. There is no reason why these various activities should not continue simultaneously, in a kind of 'parallel processing'. If the metaphor we have to live by is one of battle, then we need to be active on several fronts at once. And we need to be prepared for a long campaign. There is no opportunity to be complacent, as political attitudes can change overnight, with a consequent loss of funding or a restatement of priorities. Because bilingual education is expensive, it is under constant threat. Conflicting ideologies (such as a policy which supports anti-immigration or English as an official language) may obtain grass-roots support which suddenly endangers a project previously thought to be safe. Throughout the 1990s, there were several reports of language support programmes becoming endangered through budgetary cuts. The Hawaiian Language Program was one such, necessitating an appeal for international support in 1995. Another was in Australia, at the end of 1998, when the Northern Territory government announced plans to phase out bilingual education for its Aboriginal communities, replacing this by English-teaching programmes.[23]

For real progress in an endangered language, it is clear that several elements need to be in place. There needs to be an indigenous community interested in obtaining help, and with a positive attitude towards language rescue. There needs to be a positive political climate, committed to the preservation of ethnic identity and cultural rights, prepared to put some money where its principles are, and where the political implications of language maintenance have been thought through. And there need to be professionals available to help with the tasks of language selection, recording, analysis, and teaching. I shall now look in more detail at what each of these elements involves.

Fostering positive community attitudes

Negative attitudes towards one's own language are surprisingly common (see chapter 3). Language-aware and well-intentioned Westerners are sometimes shocked to encounter a community whose members do not care about the survival of its language, or who are antipathetic about its maintenance. How should we react, faced with such an attitude? Should we take the view that the decision is theirs alone, that we have no right to interfere in a

---

[23] See the reports in *Iatiku* 1 (1995), 3; *Ogmios* 10 (1998), 8.

situation about which, in the nature of things, we can have only a limited understanding? Or should we adopt a broader outlook, allowing our knowledge of the long-term linguistic issues involved to justify continued interest in their language and warrant attempts to change their minds? This has been a hotly debated question,[24] raising issues of great complexity and sensitivity. It is essential to 'take a view' about it, for it will influence decision-making about the provision of support. Given that there are so many languages in need of help, one argument goes, then the limited resources should be directed towards those communities whose members *are* interested in preservation; if other communities want to commit linguistic suicide, that is their own business, and we should not waste our time, energy, and money trying to persuade them otherwise.

The first thing we should recognize is that, in real life, the issues are not so black-and-white. Within a community, attitudes will be mixed: some members will be in favour of preservation, others will be against it. There will be pride, apathy, guilt, denial, regret, and many other emotions. Moreover, the reasons for support and opposition will be mixed. One family may be particularly proud of its tradition of ethnic identity; another family may not. One family may have gained a great deal economically from shifting to the new language; another family may not. One person may view an ancestral language as useless and irrelevant; another may not use functional arguments

---

[24] A defence of the former view was presented in a discussion note by Ladefoged (1992). This in turn was responded to by Dorian (1993). Several of the arguments are alluded to below.

at all, seeing it rather as a source of spiritual or psychological strength. An early goal, in assessing an endangered situation, accordingly, is to understand the reason for any negative attitudes encountered, to determine how typical they are in the community as a whole, and to evaluate the impact of the attitudes on the community's way of life, in both the short and the long term.

Some attitudes, it has to be accepted, are negative for the best of reasons. It is axiomatic that physical wellbeing is a top priority: there is no point in going on to people about language if they are too ill to speak or too hungry to listen. If food, welfare, and work are lacking, then it is only to be expected that they will direct their energies to ways of increasing resources and fostering economic growth. The same applies if military conflict, political oppression, or civil disturbance threaten their daily safety and survival. Matthew McDaniel is one field worker who has made this point, in relation to the Akha of Thailand; his language is emotive and dramatic, but it only reflects a reality:[25]

what these people need is plain old help, so they can keep their babies alive so that the babies will live long enough to learn the language ... One struggles to find out why the infants die so fast, before you could get back with medicine; there is no one to do autopsies to find out the actual cause of the death, so one is still in the dark and it happens like clockwork, and you wonder whether it matters at all if you get the language written into a dictionary when you have to look at that baby girl of three months dead on the floor of the hut and feel so damn helpless over and over again.

[25] McDaniel (1998: 15).

Unless the people in the west open up their wallets and time to give these people real help, as long as the western economic model rolls on consuming everything in sight broken down into consumption units, I think there is no hope at all and all of this work becomes foolishness.

Mari Rhydwen makes a similar point:[26]

When basic needs for shelter, food, safety and health are unmet, even thinking about language maintenance or revival seems like an irrelevant luxury.

Such observations seem almost unanswerable. And yet, it is a fact of life that circumstances, priorities, and goals all change with time. If the development programmes fostered by international organizations are at all successful, then the hope is that there will come a time when, healthy and well-fed, people will have the time and energy to devote to quality, as opposed to quantity, of life. At that point, they will look to revive their cultural traditions and to affirm their cultural identity. That is when they will look for their language. And if their language has gone, unrecorded and unremembered, there is no way in which they can get it back. By contrast, if a modicum of effort has been devoted to language preservation, even in the most difficult of economic circumstances, at least these people have kept their options open. They can make their choice, whether we are thinking about this generation, or a generation ahead.[27]

---

[26] Rhydwen (1998:105).

[27] Sociology has provided various ways of characterizing social priorities and expectations: for example, Maslow's (1954) hierarchy of social needs recognizes 'physiological > safety > belonging > esteem >self-actualization'. For an application to language, see Walker (1993).

This is the kind of argument we must use, when faced with opposition to efforts to preserve endangered languages – even when the opposition comes from the people themselves. It is also the argument that must be used when people say that outsiders have no right to intervene, especially those who come from former colonialist countries. As we shall see below, it is often not easy deciding what can and should be done to preserve a language in circumstances where the people either do not care about it or are actively pursuing alternative goals (such as the learning of English – see p. 17). There are sensitivities to be respected, and political pressures to take into account. At the same time, outsiders can often see, in a way that insiders cannot, the merits of a long-term view. They know very well, from experiences the world over, that one of the loudest complaints to eventually emerge is of the 'if only' type: 'if only my parents had ...'; 'if only my grandparents' generation had ...' Nicholas Ostler puts it this way, reacting to the view that, if a people choose not to pass their language on to the next generation, it is their choice, and who are we to dispute it?[28]

My own answer is that [any] view of the world which makes this gross analysis is itself too static, and in many cases, too complacent. Not only languages, but people are very various, and their aims and aspirations are various too. At some points in their history, members of a community may opt to give up their language, and try to move closer to other communities by adopting a common lingua franca. Often, they are pursuing a perceived, reasonable, economic goal. The problem comes when that goal changes, or perhaps when the goal is achieved,

[28] Ostler (1996: 1). The reference is to Ladefoged (1992).

and so no longer important. There is no path back: an option or an identity which was given by the old language is no longer there.

Nancy Dorian provides a specific example, arising out of her experience working among the last few Gaelic-speaking East Sutherland people of Scotland.[29] She observed the discomfort and hostility shown by some of these speakers, 'who wanted nothing more than to be inconspicuous', when they had an encounter with a Gaelic-language revivalist. Alluding to the issue raised by Peter Ladefoged – who had observed a Dahalo speaker in Kenya apparently pleased that his sons now spoke only Swahili, and who asked in his article 'Who am I to say that he was wrong?' – she commented:

The Gaelic-speaking East Sutherland fisherfolk have in one sense already been proven 'wrong', in that some of the youngest members of their own kin circles have begun to berate them for choosing not to transmit the ancestral language and so allowing it to die.

This kind of reaction is very common among the members of a community two generations after the one which failed to pass its language on.[30] The first generation is typically not so concerned, as its members are often still struggling to establish their new social position and new language. It is their children, secure in the new language and in a much better socio-economic position, with battles over land-claims and civil rights behind them,

---

[29] Dorian (1993); see also Dorian (1981).
[30] The native languages of southeast Alaska provide another example: see Dauenhauer and Dauenhauer (1998: 60).

who begin to reflect on the heritage they have lost, and to wish that things had been otherwise. The old language, formerly a source of shame, comes to be seen as a source of identity and pride. But by then, without any preservation measures, it is too late.

It is crucial that people become more widely aware of this sequence of events, simply because there are hundreds of cases already known where a community, some way along the road towards cultural assimilation (see p. 103), has come to hold strongly negative attitudes towards its ethnic language. Its members need to realize the effect of these attitudes on their descendants, who will not be in any position to choose. While therefore affirming the right of the local community to make its own decision, outsiders still have a valuable role to play in ensuring that it is an informed decision. It must all be very carefully handled, as we are living in an intellectual climate where issues of human rights and self-determination have come to rank highly in any thinking about intervention. But a policy of total non-intervention in indigenous affairs, however well-intentioned, would be a blatant disregard of the realities of history. However much we might condemn the political policies of our ancestors, we have to live with the consequences of their actions, and whether we see our present role as a form of reparation, or penance, or an affirmation of common humanity, or something else, it is far too easy to evade responsibility by saying 'leave well alone; it is their problem'. The world does not react in this way when faced with situations of famine or disease; there, the value of sensitive intervention is not in doubt. Numerous aid programmes are based on the assumption that standards of living can be improved through education. And I see no essential difference in educational programmes designed to remove ignorance about, say, water-management or pest-control, and awareness-raising designed to remove ignorance about language.

Even in a community where there seem to be no major ideological confrontations, where the people *are* concerned about their language, and where Western workers have accepted the principle of self-determination, the need to eliminate ignorance may still be urgent. For it is a fact that people on the whole *are* extraordinarily unaware about the nature of language – and here I am not talking only about indigenous peoples. Major areas of contemporary linguistics (for example, in sociolinguistics and educational linguistics), as well as many popular language initiatives in broadcasting and the press, have emerged as part of a concern to combat this lack of awareness.[31] The phenomenon of language endangerment is no exception. I am not here referring to differences in world view. If it is part of a group's beliefs that it is God's (or their god's) will that their language should die, then many people would accept that there is little outsiders can or should do (unless, of course, there is a commitment to intervention for different ideological reasons – as in the case of missionary and political activities). Similarly, if a group believes that language death is a natural evolutionary process, they may well feel strongly that it would be unnatural for humans to interfere with it, and outsiders would have to respect that belief. There are

---

[31] For a recent British example, see Bauer and Trudgill (1998); for a recent US example, see Wheeler (1999).

several other mindsets which involve considerations of a similarly fundamental kind, which would make it difficult or impossible for linguists to intervene with any success. If an indigenous community believes that all Europeans are inherently evil, acquisitive, or seeking to dominate, or that all proposals about intervention ultimately come from the CIA, then the chances of working on the language as such are distant. The issues are no less problematic when they involve social constraints governing interaction – such as when it is believed that white teachers cannot possibly understand an indigenous situation, or that women cannot be allowed to teach men.

On the other hand, there are many matters to do with language awareness which do not involve such fundamental issues. In particular, most people are totally unaware of the stages through which a language passes as it becomes increasingly endangered. They do not know just how quickly a bilingual community can become monolingual. They do not know about the phenomenon of rapid, catastrophic language shift (see chapter 1). They do not see the tell-tale signs, such as the growth in bilingualism, or the gradual increase in loan-words from the dominant language. They look around them, see others still speaking the language, and conclude that the language is strong, and that 'someone out there knows the stories'. They may deny that there are few speakers left. They say they prefer the indigenous language, and use it themselves a great deal. They refuse to accept that their language is 'endangered', 'vanishing', 'dying' – indeed, they may object most strongly to having such labels used about them at all, perceiving them to be a denial of their ethnicity (instead of just a statement about language).

They may believe that their language is under special protection.[32] It can therefore come as a shock when a survey shows few speakers and a widespread use of the dominant language.[33] It has been noted that a community may not see the need for action until it is too late to save the language.[34] Linguistic surveys have often provided precisely this inducement to action.

Or again, the people may be unaware of exactly what they are doing when they are saving a language, and what the consequences of language loss are. We need to remind ourselves, at this point, that the immediate reason for working with endangered languages is not primarily to provide people from different generations with a means of talking to each other; they very likely already have that, in the form of the dominant language (such as English or Spanish) by which they have begun to be bilingual. Rather, the initial aim is to help a community discover what is unique about its heritage. And the

---

[32] Quesada (1998: 57) reports an interview with the king of the Teribes people of Panama, whose language, in his estimation, is highly endangered. The king states plainly: 'We are not endangered', and when asked why he is so optimistic, adds: 'Because we know we are creatures of God and God has not created us to be destroyed by others. Let's face it: if we have not been exterminated along these 500 years, under worse conditions, extinction at present is highly unlikely. The Indian Autonomy Law [of 1968] is a written document. The same is true about the language.'

[33] Examples of these reactions are reported for Mohawk and Quechua: see Jacobs (1998: 118), Grinevald (1998: 139).

[34] For example, McKay (1996: 18), 'Unfortunately the stronger the language the more likely it is that the speakers will not see the need for action or the potential consequences of loss until it is too late'; Trosterud (1997: 23), 'A bilingual society can change into a monolingual assimilated one very fast, without fluent speakers realising what is going on until it is too late.'

enormity of this task must not be underestimated. It takes some effort to become consciously aware of what one's linguistic heritage contains. Living 'inside' a language, it is not possible to see its distinctiveness. So much is unnoticed and taken for granted – forms of social inter-action, everyday ritual behaviours, activities that belong to particular times of the year. People need help to think it all out, especially if they do not belong to an intellectual tradition which values the encyclopedic systematization of knowledge. The scale of the problem can be sensed from a thought experiment: imagine that English is an endangered language, and that we have to identify those of its achievements and practices which it is essential to preserve for our children. It is difficult to know where to begin.[35] We would have to select from the literary canon – reminiscent of the surviving community in Ray Bradbury's *Fahrenheit 451*, where each person committed a work to memory. We would need to find ways of capturing the core of our religious and legal language. We would need to make selections from public oratory and the media. We would not want to forget the language of our celebratory rituals, such as birthday greetings and Christmas carols, nor our interaction with children, through nursery rhymes and language games. All this, and much more, would have to be considered. And all this, and much more, has to be considered when we approach an endangered language. For what languages

[35] Another way of assessing the linguistic distinctiveness of a heritage is by examining the coverage of an encyclopedia which has a brief for a particular culture, such as Hook (1982) or the forthcoming *Encyclopedia of Wales* (Welsh Academy).

have to tell us about their heritage is of the same character everywhere.

Several myths may need to be dispelled, in order to foster the right climate for language maintenance. Some are to do with teaching. For example, there is a widespread belief that being a fluent parent is an automatic qualification for being a good classroom teacher. Another is that only teachers from the same ethnic group can teach that group's language. Other myths are to do with learning. Because learning a language as a mother tongue is so natural, unconscious, and rapid, people readily assume that older children will find it no different if the same language has to be learned artificially in a school, immersion summer camp, or adult class. They will just 'pick it up'. Ethnic reasoning may be used to reinforce this view. The adult native speakers may believe that, if children have the same ethnic background as themselves, the task of learning their language as a second language will inevitably be simple (the so-called 'genetic fallacy'). The fact of the matter, of course, is that all children learning an ancestral language as a second language in a tutored setting have to work hard to achieve success, regardless of their ethnicity. A few weeks of immersion will not do it. And even if language is being taught routinely in school, there needs to be reinforcement from the home or local community. If people are not aware of this, they will develop false expectations of success, and, when these fail to be realized, their negative attitudes will inevitably be reinforced.

It is by no means easy to help people see the consequences of negative attitudes towards language maintenance, or to eradicate myths about the process. But if it is axiomatic that a community is ultimately responsible for making its own decisions about the matter, then they should make this decision with all the facts available, insofar as they are known. They should have had a chance to think through the consequences. The important issue is choice, as Ken Hale asserts:[36]

> To reverse language loss, ultimately, a certain condition must prevail. In a word, people must have the *choice* of learning or transmitting the local language of their family, or other relevant social unit.

And he later adds:

> The condition which must prevail in order to halt language loss is a form of sociopolitical and economic justice in which this choice is not limited. This necessary condition does not obtain in any country I know about.

Choice is indeed critical – but it must be informed choice. It is no solution giving parents the right to make choices about the linguistic future of their children if they do not have the information they need on which to base that choice. And enabling people to see the arguments for language maintenance, without minimizing the difficulties involved in any commitment, is an important early step in working with a community whose language is endangered, and where there is distrust about the process. This is where linguists and others can play an important role. Only the indigenous community itself can save its language. But that still leaves plenty for outsiders to do, by way of advice and help.

[36] Hale (1998: 213, 215).

Linguists working with endangered languages thus have a very clear task ahead of them, when they encounter negative attitudes towards an ancestral language among the members of an indigenous community. An early aim of intervention must be to create opportunities for the people to improve morale so that they come to think of their language with feelings of confidence, self-esteem, and pride. Only in this way will the community develop an ability from within to deal with the pressure of ongoing change. As one group of researchers has put it: 'The decision to abandon one's own language always derives from a change in the self-esteem of the speech community.'[37] So, how can a community boost its confidence in its own language? There is little hope for a language unless its speakers feel that it is worth continuing with. But what kind of arguments instil a sense of worth, if that has been steadily eroded by years of contempt? Arising out of the experience of working with several communities, linguists have developed a sense of which issues can be persuasive – though there is never, of course, a guarantee that the next community will be swayed by them. The situation is not dissimilar to that found in preventive medicine: knowing the right way forward is one thing; persuading people to take it is another. It is the same with preventive linguistics, where the disease to be annihilated is that of linguistic apathy or despair.

With some peoples, the simple fact that they are bilingual – either because they always were, or because they have come to be so as a result of contact with the dominant language – is seen as a real advantage (see p. 59).

[37] Brenzinger, Heine, and Somner (1991: 37).

Despite their relatively low status, they perceive the limitations of the monolingual condition. The ability to speak more than one language is considered a source of prestige and power in several communities: reported examples include the Emenyo of New Guinea and the Arizona Tewa. There are moreover many circumstances in which an indigenous language can be of practical value – for example, being used as a common language between countries which have different majority languages (an example would be a Bantu language linking South Africa and Mozambique). Such a language can also be extremely useful as a private channel of communication within the indigenous community – one which the dominant group does not share.[38] Many of the positive arguments can come only from the members of the community themselves. Only they can point to the psychological or spiritual gains which come from having links with an ancestral language – gains which are intangible, but nonetheless real, such as the delight which accompanies the reading of old writings, or hearing old tales, and the feelings of security which are generated by a sense of identity and history.

Art is another major way of boosting self-esteem, through the promotion of story-telling sessions, drama groups, poetry readings, public-speaking competitions, singing galas, and cultural gatherings, such as the eisteddfod tradition in Wales, or the Mod festivals in Gaelic-speaking Scotland. A strong literary tradition can be a

---

[38] Of course, this possibility is precisely one of the reasons why the dominant group might have tried to eliminate the indigenous language in the first place: see pp. 107–8. See also Wurm (1991: 15).

source of great prestige, not only within the indigenous community but also among the society at large. Even in the case of art forms where there is no linguistic element, such as dancing, language can take advantage of their popularity: no dance has yet been invented which has not been given a name or an interpretation, and language then comes to the fore. But, in talking about art forms, it is crucial to include all sectors of society. In a situation of endangerment, there is no room for a misconceived elitism or anti-elitism. There has to be inclusiveness, simply because not everyone in the endangered community will find everything equally appealing. The critical dimension is age. The kind of activities promoted by the long-established cultural festivals can appear old-fashioned or parochial to the community's youth. On the other hand, the kind of activity which interests the young can be dismissed by the older generation as involving a lowering of standards. Without mutual interest and tolerance, a community can find itself torn by internal conflict, and energies which should be harnessed in the same direction come to be dissipated.

A classic example of a wasted moment took place in Wales in 1998, when the world-renowned Welsh pop group, Manic Street Preachers, used the Welsh language on an enormous sheet hung on the outside of an office-block in Cardiff to advertise their new album, *This is My Truth – Tell Me Yours (Dyma'n ngwirionedd – Dwêd un ti)*. The members of the group do not speak Welsh, but, as their spokesperson put it, 'They wanted to do something special for Wales' because 'They are very proud of their Welsh heritage.' Such a gesture is offered so rarely to a language under threat, and one would have expected it to receive appropriate media attention. So it did. 'Manic Street Preachers' bad language upsets the land of their fathers' read the headline in the *Independent* (27 September 1998). The reason was that the language used had been condemned by one Welsh academic as:

pidgin Welsh and grammatically incorrect ... It should be, 'Dwêd dy un ti.' ... It's slang ... the language is being allowed to deteriorate. It's an eyesore. Standards are not being kept up.

A spokesman for the Welsh Language Board put up a robust defence:

We welcome the fact that the Manic Street Preachers have produced such a massive banner in the medium of Welsh which reflects popular youth culture ... A lot of teenagers are learning Welsh now, and gestures like these make them proud to be Welsh and to be able to speak the language.

Another journalist, in the *Daily Post*, used rather more vivid language:

Professor Busybody is defending 'correct' Welsh, keeping it safe in the cosy confines of the Cardiff middle class. The rest of us are left to rue over a lost opportunity to change the perception of the language among young English-speakers of South Wales. The banner stunt was publicity that money can't buy, but the pedantic prof got in the way.

And he concludes, along with the Welsh Language Board, 'The Manic Street Preachers got it right.'

The age-group in question is critical for the future of Welsh. Although recent censuses show growth in the language's use at certain ages, the teenage years remain a source of concern. In a word, many teenagers (who will be the parents of the next generation) do not find it 'cool' to speak Welsh. With such a prestigious role model, this attitude might have begun to be reversed. For some Welsh elders not to have seen this is a serious problem for the future of the language. Ironically, one of the factors which can hasten the death of a language is the conflicts generated from within the community by those who hold different attitudes towards it. It can tear a small community apart. I have lost count of the number of people in Wales who would otherwise be sympathetic to Welsh who have been put off the language by the attitudes of language extremists. The last straw for one local councillor, Welsh in all respects except language (see further below), was when he arrived at a local government office in Gwynedd, North Wales, to hand in a report. He put it down on the officer's desk. The officer looked at him, and asked him whether he had forgotten that Gwynedd had a bilingual policy. The councillor was puzzled, replying that his report was indeed bilingual, English on one side, Welsh on the other. 'But', returned the officer, 'you have put it down English-side-up.' People with an intelligent approach to language maintenance raise their eyes in despair, when they hear such stories. They are, unfortunately, all too common.

None of this is restricted to Welsh. Reports from many endangered situations bear witness to such conflicts, where the older generation views the younger one as not speaking the 'proper' language, and where language enthusiasts adopt views which actually do harm to their cause through their narrow vision. The issues are evidently general ones of some importance, and they need to be explored. First, faced with an increasingly endangered language, and assuming there is a motivation to save it, then what form of the language is to be passed on? How does one decide what is authentic? And second, the broader issue: what does it mean to be part of an indigenous community? Is language an obligatory part of an indigenous culture, and what kind of attention should be paid to it?

Promoting the authenticity of the whole community

The linguist's response to the first set of questions is unequivocal: the *whole* of a language is authentic, in all its dialects, varieties, and styles. It is an axiom of linguistics that all languages change, as they keep pace with society;[39] and one of the consequences of this change is the proliferation of new words, pronunciations, grammatical patterns, discourse styles, and regional or social varieties, alongside the gradual loss of older forms of expression. There is an inevitable coexistence of new forms and old, in any language, and these come to be distributed about the society in relation to such factors as the age, sex, social class, and profession of the speakers. There is an important parallel, in this respect, between thriving languages and endangered languages. Indeed, English – the healthiest language of all, numerically – is well recognized for the range of its varieties (p. 12) and for its readiness to take in new words from languages with which it comes into contact (p. 45). The true life of any

---

[39] Aitchison (1991). For a poetic comment, Louis MacNeice: 'the formula fails that fails to make it clear / That only change prevails, that the seasons make the year' ('Plurality', 1940).

language is found in the breadth of its variation and its readiness to change, to adapt itself to new circumstances. The only languages which do not change are dead ones. The message for endangered languages is clear: its speakers need to be prepared for change. It is not as if they have any choice in the matter. Even though the elders in a community will be naturally conservative in their attitudes, there is nothing they can do to stop linguistic change. Some of the changes may well be unpalatable to them – in particular, the introduction of 'alien' words from the dominant language, or of colloquial styles of speech. But to accept new forms into a language does not entail the replacement of all older forms of expression, any more than the arrival of a new style of music eradicates everything that went before. A more accurate perspective is to think of the language as expanding, while it assimilates the new forms. The respected language of old rituals and literatures can still be retained, alongside whatever novelties are being introduced. Native equivalents can be coined (often by language committees) to provide equivalents for the borrowed words from the dominant language.[40] The canon of such languages as modern English or Spanish contains a vast array of older forms of expression, in such domains as religion, law, and literature, alongside the more recent innovations. Endangered languages may be much smaller in scale, but they can in principle achieve the same range of expressiveness.

---

[40] Traditional methods of word formation can be used to express modern concepts. An example is seen in a project on Hupa, a Californian language, where strategies found to be common in the formation of long-established words were used to create new ones: see Ahlers and Hinton (1997: 18).

There is of course one fundamental difference between a major international language and an endangered language, and that is to do with the notion of ownership.[41] There comes a point in the spread of a language when no one can be said to own it – in the sense of having a recognized right to direct its development. No one 'owns' English now. Although there was a time when the British 'owned' it, through its historical connection, English is now used in so many places by so many people that it no longer has a single centre of influence. By contrast, within a very small community, the influence of a few individuals, or a local committee, can be extensive. It is therefore critical for an indigenous community to adopt an appropriately flexible and inclusive attitude towards language variation, especially in relation to the forms used by younger people, if they do not want to alienate large sections of their society from the task of language maintenance. They have to recognize that, even though the language has changed from its traditional character, it can nonetheless be of great psychological and social value as a means of providing people with a badge of identity. This is one of the most difficult mindsets to adopt, especially when people have been part of a tradition which sees the ancestral language as sacred or pure. But if they continue to think of linguistic borrowing as a sign of limited language competence, if their teachers reject variations in each others' usage as unauthentic, if elders see the usage of young people as a dilution, then the prospects are not

[41] There are several concepts of ownership. Two others are discussed in chapter 5.

good.[42] An unyielding, condemnatory purism is the worst possible scenario for language survival.

It is prerequisite for language survival for the whole – or, at least, a significant majority – of a community to be involved; and this means that everyone has to develop a sense of responsibility for language transmission. The point seems a straightforward one; but in fact there is often some uncertainty over who is actually responsible for 'saving' a language. People may be very ready to agree that their language needs to be maintained, but do not feel that they themselves have to be involved; they expect others to do it for them. They think that an organization, such as a foundation, a school, or a preservation society, will perform the necessary miracle. 'Let's leave it to the teachers', is a common observation. This is what two Alaskan fieldworkers, Nora and Richard Dauenhauer, have called the 'bureaucratic fix'.[43] But there is no such fix. Institutions cannot replace individuals. School programmes, no matter how excellent, cannot replace home-based activities. The Dauenhauers put it this way:

Sealaska Heritage Foundation, where we are employed, can contribute staff expertise in Tlingit literacy, applied folklore and linguistics, and book production; but we still require the talent, cooperation, and good will of the individual tradition bearers. We can provide professional consultation and technical training for communities, but people must want it first. We can document the stories, but we cannot create them out of

---

[42] These are all attitudes reported in the literature, for example by Yamamoto (1998a: 220).
[43] Dauenhauer and Dauenhauer (1998: 69–70).

nothing; we can produce grammars and instructional material, but they are nothing unless people actually speak the language to each other in the home and community.

The Dauenhauers also identify the readiness with which people look for a 'technical fix' – a new computer program perhaps, or a set of recordings, or some new materials that will 'save the language'. In fact, they point out, in several places there are already enough materials prepared to teach the language for a long time; the problem is finding teachers who can use them (see below).

An appropriate bureaucracy and technology are important aids in fostering language maintenance, but they can never be its foundation. The foundation must come from within the homes and neighbourhoods of the community members themselves. In an ideal situation, everyone plays a part: young parents actively discuss priorities; their older counterparts, with more experience and social standing, use their influence to give language measures a greater public voice; the elderly act as sources for the language and as role-models in its use. People who are part of the wider community also have a role to play. Their positive support for an indigenous language can give its speakers a feeling of worth, and boost their efforts to maintain it. And even rejection and antagonism from outsiders can have a positive effect, resulting in the growth of a determination and activism which might otherwise be lacking. Indeed, some analysts have argued that too much outside support can actually be harmful to an endangered language, in that it might undermine the indigenous community's motivation and sense of self-sufficiency.

Seeing language as part of culture

The second set of questions raised above now need to be addressed: what does it mean to be part of an indigenous community? Is language an obligatory part of an indigenous culture, and what kind of attention should be paid to it? Much of the discussion so far has taken the notion of 'indigenous community' for granted. It assumes that everyone knows what that community is, and who belongs to it.[44] In fact, membership can be a hotly contested issue, especially when a language shift has been going on for some time. Broadly speaking, there are two positions to be considered.

The first position asserts that there is considerable identity between language and the culture of which it is a part. Its supporters accept the arguments of chapter 2, that language expresses their identity and their history, and make this the chief consideration. In their view, so much of their culture is expressed in language that it is not possible to be a member of their community if one does not speak its language. The outcome, of course, is that people who no longer speak the language, or who have never spoken it, are excluded from the culture, even if on other grounds they believe themselves to be part of it. This position is more likely to be espoused by people who do speak the indigenous language. It sees language as an *obligatory* feature of ethnicity.

The second position asserts that there is only a limited identity between language and culture. Its supporters see far more elements in culture than language. In their view, it is possible for people to be members of an indigenous community

---

[44] And 'culture', too. However, the argument of this book does not depend on affirming any one theory of culture, but needs only to recognize that, whichever cultural theory we adopt, 'language always plays an important part': see the conclusion of Duranti (1997: 49).

even if they do not speak its language, or speak it in a very different form (cf. above), because these other elements provide the basis of their cultural identity. This position is more likely to be espoused by people who do not speak the indigenous language. It sees language as an *optional* feature of ethnicity.

Nancy Dorian provides a real example of this argument from her work in Scotland:[45]

> I found that when I asked speakers of Scottish Gaelic whether a knowledge of Gaelic was necessary to being a 'true Highlander', they said it was; when I asked people of Highland birth and ancestry who did not speak Gaelic the same question, they said it wasn't.

I have frequently encountered the same responses in Wales, where as many as 80% of the people do not speak the language.[46] And the split in opinion seems to be found everywhere. The Dauenhauers found it in Alaska, for example, where 90% of the Tlingit people do not speak the language.[47] They provide a telling anecdote:

> We heard an extreme example of one elder publically condemning as not being genuinely Tlingit all those young people who don't speak Tlingit. The irony is that the children, grandchildren, and great-grandchildren of this woman do not speak Tlingit. Without thinking, this woman is essentially disavowing her own family for an aspect of their ethnic identity she is responsible in part for creating.

Faced with such a deep-rooted controversy, it is once again necessary to 'take a view'. We cannot but be

---

[45] Dorian (1998: 20).
[46] See also Bourhis, Giles, and Tajfel (1974), James (1977).
[47] Dauenhauer and Dauenhauer (1998: 74, 76).

impressed by the fact that there can be so many people in an indigenous community who believe that they are part of that community even though they do not speak its ancestral language, and who manifest their sense of identity by the other choices they make in their appearance and behaviour. This is primary evidence that it is possible to retain some degree of identity without relying on language. Indeed, not all cultures, according to some reports, seem to have the same regard for language as a potent symbol of ethnic identity. Matthias Brenzinger and his colleagues have reported some instances from Africa. In one paper, they describe the behaviour of several Serer men from Senegal who had replaced their language with Wolof:[48]

Nevertheless, they turned out to be ardent adherents of Serer culture and ethnic identity, who described Wolof culture as being 'inferior' to their own in almost all respects, insisting that they would do everything possible in order to defend Serer culture against Wolof domination. The fact that none of them was able to speak the Serer language was for them quite irrelevant.

Anecdotes like this underline the point that culture is multifaceted, containing thousands of elements, many of which have nothing directly to do with language, belonging to such domains as clothing, hairstyle, food, dance, crafts, and the visual arts. It is perfectly normal for people to use these as 'badges of ethnicity', whether or not they control the associated ethnic language. They see

---

[48] Brenzinger, Heine, and Somner (1991: 37). A similar point is made for East Africa by Dimmendaal (1989: 28).

language as just one of the badges available to them. Because of its complexity and pervasiveness in society, of course, language is widely acknowledged as the behaviour with the greatest potential to act as a badge (see chapter 2);[49] but it is not the only way that culture can be transmitted. Culture does not come to a complete stop, when any one of its elements changes or ceases to exist, even when that is language. The loss of a language is certainly the nearest thing to a serious heart attack that a culture can suffer. But people can survive heart attacks; and so can cultures.

The overwhelming evidence is that there can be cultural continuity despite language shift.[50] The new culture is not the same as the old, of course, but it is not totally different either. The outstanding question, which research has hardly begun to elucidate, is to establish what the differences are – to determine what is retained and what is lost, from a cultural point of view, when language shift takes place. Which elements of the old language can be taken over by the new, without significant cultural loss? On the one hand, it is clearly possible to tell the old stories through the medium of the new language, and much of the old lore and wisdom can still be explained

---

[49] People do not usually dare to make a quantitative estimate, which is why the reference to 'two-thirds of a people's culture is bound up in their language', made by a Mohawk leader, is especially interesting: see MacDougall (1998: 91).

[50] This dynamic view of culture, in which ethnicity is seen as a continuum along which elements are constantly being renegotiated over time, is a theme of Dauenhauer and Dauenhauer (1998), and also emerges in several other papers in the Grenoble and Whaley volume (1998), notably those by Jocks, Mithun, and Woodbury. Identity is seen as dynamic, changing, ongoing, and not restricted to traditional practices.

and discussed in it. On the other hand, a great deal will be lost in the translation: the new language will be unable to convey the same warmth or spirit of the stories, word-play will be missing, anecdotes and jokes will lack a certain punch, ceremonial expressions will not have the same alliterative or rhythmical gravity. But these are familiar points about the limitations of translation, applicable to all languages. The fact remains that, in exactly the same way as we can learn a great deal about French life, culture, and thought from works translated out of French, it is possible to obtain from a dominant language some of the cultural weight of the endangered language it is in the process of replacing. Anthony Woodbury puts it this way:[51]

a language of wider communication (such as English) can be adapted ideologically, if not always structurally, to communicative ends that are continuous with those earlier fulfilled by an ancestral language.

A view of language as a pre-eminent but not exclusive badge of ethnicity provides the most promising basis for the maintenance of an endangered language. If a community works with it, or can be persuaded to work with it, this view allows for a *modus vivendi* between those who are monolingual in the indigenous language, those who are in varying degrees bilingual, those who are semilingual, and those who are monolingual in the dominant language. And because involvement in ethnicity means participation in shared cultural practices, gains in language use are likely. Not everyone will opt for complete ownership of the language badge; but everyone will be part of an ethos

[51] Woodbury (1998: 235).

in which the language badge is held in positive regard, and where some level of active command – even if only at the level of daily greetings or use of street names – is virtually unavoidable.

This approach also allows for a further kind of inclusiveness, when we encounter people who no longer live in the indigenous community yet still wish to be a part of it. The circumstances vary greatly, from optional emigration to forced displacement, but the end result is the same: there may be significant numbers who live abroad, some of whom speak the ancestral language while some do not, who wish to retain or rediscover their indigenous heritage. With some ethnic groups, the issue is global in scope, for waves of emigration may have been taking place to widely dispersed settings over many years. The notion of 'heritage' has sometimes been used to provide a bridge between the concern over ethnicity which we find in a homeland setting and that which we find among communities of immigrants, refugees, and other displaced people scattered throughout the world.[52] It is not a particularly homogeneous concept, for it includes (for example) small indigenous groups undergoing cultural assimilation within their own country (such as the various Amerindian peoples), large groups of recent immigrants in a foreign city (such as the Chinese or Italians in London or Boston), and ethnic groups for whom the 'homeland' is a distant memory (as in the turning towards Africa of many African Americans in the USA). The kind of language these people associate with their sense of heritage will often be unclear – which African language? Which Chinese

[52] Van Deusen-Scholl (1998).

language? Which Italian dialect? Even when it *is* clear, there will be a wide range of linguistic abilities present, from total fluency in the heritage language to retaining only a 'heritage accent'. But a genuinely comprehensive model of language endangerment has to allow for these circumstances too. It is by no means just an academic question. Important levels of support for a homeland situation can come from abroad. And in cases where an endangered language has had many of its speakers dispersed, it is a real – and often highly contentious – question of whether to offer support to all groups, wherever they live, or to concentrate support in the homeland only.

Taking a view about the role of language in culture is also important for another reason: it motivates decisions about where support for a language is best directed. If a community adopts the *obligatory* view, it will expect revitalization to be focused on matters directly to do with language – language-teaching resources and training, for example, and the range of linguistic activities to be described in chapter 5. If it adopts the *optional* view, it will expect revitalization to be focused on matters to do with the culture – providing social welfare, for example, or introducing measures to boost the economy. In an ideal world, a balance would be found between these two pressures, so that they would not be in inevitable confrontation. In practice, limited funding means that projects relating to each view are often in competition for the same resources; nor may there be sufficient local expertise in language planning to analyse the long-term consequences of a decision in the community. The perspective which is most prominent in sociolinguistics advocates a 'culture-first' view: language maintenance will be most efficient, in the long term, if one begins by providing support for the cultural milieu or matrix within which that language is found, and from which people will draw their motivation to use it. Promoting the culture as a whole is the best precondition for enabling a language to grow.

The 'culture-first' view is not without its difficulties – not least, the question of deciding which aspects of culture should be recognized as relevant to language maintenance. Just how much of a country's civilization can be legitimately included under the heading of a 'language revitalization' campaign? The issue can be the source of heated controversy. For example, the Academy of Mayan Languages was criticized in 1992 for devoting a great deal of effort to a project to do with reforestation.[53] Critics argued that an economic programme of this kind was so far removed from language – and even from culture – that it was an inappropriate use of resources. The limited funds should have been focused more directly on language-related activities which met the immediate demand for help. Supporters argued that economic measures of this kind would eventually lead to an increase in the community's power and prestige, thereby placing its language on a stronger footing. There is plainly truth on both sides. On the one hand, economics, as Lenore Grenoble and Lindsay Whaley conclude, 'may be the single strongest force influencing the fate of endangered languages'.[54] On the other hand, the language 'badge' may be so important, locally, that people who lack it

[53] England (1998: 107).   [54] Grenoble and Whaley (1998b: 52).

may feel seriously deprived, and demand urgent remedial action. This kind of reaction would be especially likely in parts of the world where language ability brings with it certain socioeconomic rights: for example, in Colombia, the ability to speak an indigenous language is part of the evidence that the government uses to decide whether a person is a member of an indigenous people, and thus entitled to such benefits as a place on a reservation, tax exemption, and free energy supply.[55]

The long-term implications of the 'culture-first' position (usually requiring significant levels of economic investment and social reform) mean that governments will often opt for the short-term 'fix', in which measures are taken to solve an immediate problem – in effect, shoring up a language where they see it most under threat. Unfortunately, the effectiveness of these measures tends to be inversely proportional to the amount of political noise which accompanies them. There is no substitute, in language maintenance, for careful, long-term forward planning, with the first priority being the promotion of a language's cultural milieu, and within which an array of short-term measures has been judiciously selected. Curiously, it is one of the hardest jobs on earth to convince a language extremist of that. A purism on behalf of an endangered language is no less stultifying than a purism on behalf of a dominant language.

It is easy to let intellectual awareness of the controversies, and political cynicism over the outcomes, eat away at any enthusiastic response to the question with which I began

---

[55] Seifart (1998: 9).

this chapter, 'Where do we begin?' If the task is to rebuild a community's self-confidence, often after several hundred years of cultural domination, anything other than a gloomy prospect seems remote. Within the community, the size of the task can be enough to put people off. They know they don't know enough. They know they haven't the resources. They therefore delay making decisions, or pick at the problem, instead of approaching it systematically. They look for quick returns, and then, when they find these do not work, they are put off once again. They underestimate the amount of preliminary work which needs to be in place before significant progress can be made. Faced, then, with a community mood which lies somewhere along the range from black to very black, it is important to draw attention to the cases where problems have been overcome, and significant progress has been made, for these have been many. It is perhaps too soon, in most instances, to talk about 'success stories', for not enough research has been done to establish the long-term impact of a few years or decades of language-shift reversal. At the same time, if long life is not yet guaranteed for these cases, there is now plenty of evidence to show that death has been postponed.

5
What can be done?

~

The preceding two chapters have raised a number of
general considerations which are involved in the early
stages of working with an endangered language. Chapter 3
drew attention to the range of factors which cause a
language to decline; chapter 4 emphasized the effect of
this process on people's attitudes. Both perspectives are
needed before we are in a position to make informed
decisions about when and how to intervene, in order to
reverse language shift – or indeed about whether
intervention is practicable or desirable.[1]

Our decisions may be informed, but they are not always
based on principles that are fully understood. There is still
so much that we do not know. What motivates the
members of a community to work for their language?
Why do some communities become so involved and others
do not? Sometimes the reasons are very clear: for example,
a powerful combination of political and religious factors
explain the rebirth and ongoing maintenance of Hebrew in

---

[1] The question of desirability raises a host of issues which have been little
discussed. Some writers are well aware of a medical analogy, and have
asked (though not answered) the same kinds of difficult question which
are encountered in medical ethics. 'Should we keep languages alive on
respirators and breathing tubes?', asks Matisoff (1991: 221), and he raises
the spectre of 'linguistic euthanasia' in cases where the community
expresses its wish for its language to be allowed to die, or rejects outside
help entirely. I do not think the subject is yet ready to provide principled
answers to such questions.

modern Israel.[2] But most endangered situations do not permit easy analysis. Nor is the range of factors and how they interact completely understood. We know a great deal about why languages become endangered and die, and why people shift from one language to another (see chapter 3), but we still know very little about why they are maintained, and why people stay loyal to them. Surprising cases of language maintenance, even in the most adverse of circumstances, are encountered. The Tewa of Arizona are an example: they have long been a small group within the dominant Hopi community, and yet their language has been strongly maintained. In trying to explain this, linguists have noted the Tewa's real concern over stylistic consistency in the use of ceremonial and religious speech, even to the extent of physically punishing anyone who might make use of non-Tewa expressions; also, a spirit of linguistic tolerance is strongly present among the Hopi.[3] But it is difficult to find ways of quantifying such notions as 'real concern over consistency' and 'strong presence of tolerance', and much of the commentary in the research literature still remains impressionistic.

In most settings, clusters of factors interact in subtle ways. A report on the Ugong of Thailand tries to explain why this language has died out in some places and not in

---

[2] However, Modern Hebrew is a very special case. Although very different from Classical Hebrew in its many European influences, there has been significant continuity in writing between classical and modern times, and also in speech through several European vernacular varieties.

[3] Kroskrity (1993). Another case of survival in an unfavourable setting is the Barbareno Chumash of California, who were taken into a Franciscan mission in the late eighteenth century, and made to learn Spanish, yet its last speaker did not die until 1965: see Mithun (1998: 183).

others. The researcher, David Bradley, concludes that the language has survived in geographical areas which are relatively isolated, the communities there being more likely to be economically self-sufficient and to have had little contact with outside groups (and thus few or no marriages to outsiders). In such places, the headman retained some measure of political control and social prestige, and there was no access to Thai-based education in schools.[4] In the case of the Maori of New Zealand, a different cluster of factors seems to have been operative, involving a strong ethnic community involvement since the 1970s, a long-established (over 150 years) literacy presence among the Maori, a government educational policy which has brought Maori courses into schools and other centres, such as the *kohanga reo* ('language nests'), and a steadily growing sympathy from the English-speaking majority. Also to be noted is the fact that Maori is the only indigenous language of the country, so that it has been able to claim the exclusive attention of those concerned with language rights.[5] In the case of Welsh, the critical factors included the rise of a strong community movement in the 1970s, the presence of a visionary leader (prepared in this case to fast to death: see p. 115), the establishment of a Welsh-medium television channel, and the passing of protective legislation (notably, the Welsh Language Acts of 1967 and 1993).[6] In the case of one project on Irish in Northern Ireland,

---

[4] Bradley (1989: 33–40).
[5] For historical background, see Benton (1996). For an analysis in terms of factors, see Grenoble and Whaley (1998b: 49ff.).
[6] See the papers in Ball (1988) and Bellin (1984).

the critical factor was a remarkable level of personal commitment, leading to the emergence of a socially dynamic community: eleven families from West Belfast undertook to learn Irish, buying houses in the same neighbourhood (Shaw's Road) and raising their children as bilinguals. The project enhanced the prestige of the language, and inspired other enterprises of this kind in the region.[7] In the case of Rama, in Nicaragua, the chief factors were reported to be the involvement of a visionary language rescuer who managed to motivate the local community, the constitutional commitment to linguistic and cultural rights which followed the Sandinista revolution, and the presence of a team of professional linguists.[8]

These are just a few of the many cases on record where individual languages have been seen to make progress in recent years.[9] In none of these cases would we yet be able to guarantee the safety of the languages in the long term. Indeed, in some instances, an objective assessment of numbers of speakers might actually show a downturn, despite a period of intense language support. This is often because of the lateness of the intervention: it can take a long time before the number of new speakers manages to exceed the death of older speakers. Also, the initial

---

[7] Maguire (1991).   [8] Craig (1992).
[9] Several other examples are given by Dorian (1998); see also the papers by Dauenhauer and Dauenhauer, England, Jacobs, and Grinevald in Grenoble and Whaley (1998a). Wurm (1998: 203ff.) reports on progress with Ainu (Japan), Djabugay (Australia), Faeroese, Tahitian, Yukagir (Siberia), and several other cases. Other reports of progress appear in the bulletins of the Foundation for Endangered Languages; illustrative are the reports on Hawaiian (*Newsletter* 1. 3), Livonian (*Iatiku* 3. 3), Cayuga and Mohawk (*Iatiku* 3. 12), Inupiak (*Newsletter* 5. 19), Salish (*Ogmios* 6. 18), and Chimila (*Ogmios* 9. 9).

enthusiasm of some language learners might wane, as they encounter the time-consuming realities of their task. And, all the time, there is the constant pressure towards language loss coming from the dominant culture in the ways outlined in chapter 3. Yet, as we read the reports from field linguists and community workers, we cannot fail to note a mood of optimism and confidence which was not present a decade ago. Trond Trosterud tells a nice story which illustrates this in relation to the Sámi (earlier called Lapp) people of northern Norway:[10]

Attending a meeting of Sámi and Norwegian officials, one of the Sámi participants was asked: do you need an interpreter? No, she answered, I don't. But I will give my talk in Sámi, so it might be that you will need one.

So, if there is now a significant body of data on language maintenance projects which have achieved some success, are there any factors which turn up so frequently that they could be recognized as postulates for a theory of language revitalization – that is, prerequisites for progress towards the goal of language being used in the home and neighbourhood as a tool of inter-generational communication?[11] I attach primary significance to six such factors.

1 An endangered language will progress if its speakers increase their prestige within the dominant community.

Prestige comes when people start to notice you. An endangered community therefore needs to make its

[10] Trosterud (1997: 24).
[11] For a profound appreciation of the whole issue, see Fishman (1991).

presence felt within the wider community. It needs to raise its visibility, or profile. Obtaining access to the media (traditionally, the province of the dominant culture) is critical – to begin with, a regular column in a daily newspaper, perhaps, or an occasional programme exposing the language on radio or television, such as a cultural celebration or a religious festival. But the media will only report what they perceive to be significant community activity, hence the first step is to enhance that activity in community settings, such as churches, social centres, and town halls. People have to get into the habit of using a language, and this requires that they have regular access to it. Sporadic language activities need to be replaced by activities in which the language has a predictable presence, thus enabling a process of consolidation to take place. Decisions need to be made about which social activities to concentrate on: after all, people cannot revitalize everything at once. Certain functions may need to be selected for special effort, such as story-telling or religious ritual. Traditional religious links and practices are especially important in the way they provide motivation for language revival, as are the arts.

The longer-term aim is to increase visibility in more and more sectors of the public domain. The worlds of business, law, and public administration are particularly important targets. A token presence is often all that can initially be obtained, through letter-headings, company symbols, and the like; but if the political circumstances are auspicious, this can steadily grow, until it becomes (as in present-day Wales) co-equal with the dominant language in such areas as advertising, public-service leaflets, and minute-taking. There is an associated growth in translation and interpreting services. With political support, also, a high level of visibility can come from the use of the indigenous language in place names, on road signs, and on public signs in general. These usually provide a real indication of the acceptability of a language's presence in the wider community, and are thus often a focus of activism.[12] The defaced road signs in many countries, in which names in the dominant language have been painted over by their Welsh, Basque, Gaelic (etc.) equivalents, provide a contemporary illustration. They demonstrate the presence of a community dynamism which has gone further than the law permits in order to express corporate linguistic identity. But dynamism at grass-roots level there must be. One contributor to an e-mail discussion put it this way:[13]

Languages are not 'objects' to be 'saved', but processes of social interaction that define particular groups. If no significant social boundaries set a group off from the ambient society, no amount of effort by linguists and educators is going to preserve a language, except as a documented artifact. But the reverse is also true. Once a social group achieves sufficient cohesion and independence ... there is no stopping language being used for identity purposes.

2 An endangered language will progress if its speakers increase their wealth relative to the dominant community

I have already quoted an observation by Grenoble and Whaley that economics 'may be the single strongest force

---

[12] *Ogmios* 6 (1997: 12ff.) carried a report of a trial of four members of a Macedonian minority party in Greece for the use of their mother tongue on a public sign.

[13] Golla (1998: 20).

influencing the fate of endangered languages' (see p. 166), but the point is so salient that it deserves to be repeated. I am inclined to agree, if for no other reason than that it costs money to raise the social and political profile of a language, and that money will only be forthcoming in a prosperous environment. But a change in economic fortunes has a more fundamental and positive impact on the self-esteem of a community, as long as the increase in prosperity is gradual, and is well managed. (There are cases, such as the oil booms in some parts of the world, where the arrival of sudden wealth has proved to be destructive of an indigenous community.) The strengthened economy of Catalonia, for example, has been a major factor in encouraging the use of Catalan there, and this has enhanced the prestige of the language in other Catalan-speaking areas. Service industries and light manufacturing industries tend to be the domains in which endangered languages can most benefit from economic growth. (By contrast, as we have seen in chapter 3, the so-called 'primary' industries of the world, and especially the extractive industries, such as mining and quarrying, have had an overall harmful effect on indigenous languages, because of the way they attract exploitation by outside organizations.)

Tourism is a good example of a service industry which can bring considerable benefits to an endangered language, as has been seen in parts of Switzerland and northern Italy. Dolomitic Ladin, for example, spoken in a few small locations in the South Tyrol, has benefited in this way, as has the use of Romansh, since 1938 one of the four national languages of Switzerland, spoken in the canton of Graubünden (Grisons) in south-east Switzerland, and also in the valleys of the upper Rhine and Inn rivers.[14] Other minority languages and dialects in the region have also developed a higher profile as a result of the tourist presence, such as Franco-Provençale in the Vallée d'Aoste, the German-related Walser in the Vallée de Gressoney, and Friulian in the extreme north-east of Italy. A significant attribute of tourists, of course, is that they come and go, at different times of the year, and represent a wide range of linguistic backgrounds. There is thus less likelihood of the emergence of an alien threatening presence in the indigenous community.

3 An endangered language will progress if its speakers increase their legitimate power in the eyes of the dominant community

The closing decades of the twentieth century saw indigenous languages in many parts of the world benefiting from a trend in public opinion displaying increased sympathy towards cultural and linguistic rights. The mood was particularly strong in Europe, where a series of statements emerged from within the leading political organizations; and while these were inevitably focused on the position of the lesser-used languages of Europe, they sent a strong message to those concerned with language rights in other parts of the world. In 1981, a milestone was passed when the European Parliament adopted a resolution, prepared by Gaetano Arfé (an Italian member of a parliamentary committee), proposing a Community

---

[14] Markey (1988). For the other languages of the region, see the various entries in Price (1998).

charter to deal with regional languages and cultures and the rights of ethnic minorities. In 1992 another milestone was reached when the Council of Europe adopted the European Charter for Regional or Minority Languages in the form of a convention; this came into force on 1 March 1998. As a convention, it is legally binding on the ratifying countries, and offers significant levels of protection for minority languages in crucial walks of life.[15] Other bodies, notably the Organization for Security and Cooperation in Europe, have contributed important statements which have helped to encourage the current climate, and the European Bureau for Lesser Used Languages, with its aim of conserving and promoting the regional, autochthonous languages and cultures of the European Union, has been a significant facilitating force.[16]

It is perhaps not surprising to see European support these days for multilingualism, given that the European Union has affirmed the national-language principle in its affairs, despite the costs involved: if a country is proud of its right to have its national language used in Brussels,

---

[15] Seven countries ratified the Charter at the outset: Croatia, Finland, Hungary, Liechtenstein, Netherlands, Norway, and Switzerland. A further eleven countries signed it (an initial step in the process towards ratification): Austria, Cyprus, Denmark, Germany, Luxembourg, Malta, Romania, Slovenia, Spain, the former Yugoslav Republic of Macedonia, and Ukraine. The UK, after several years of prevarication, finally agreed to sign later in 1998. Measures of protection are given to education (Article 8), judicial authorities (9), administrative authorities and public services (10), media (11), cultural activities and facilities (12), economic and social life (13), and transfrontier exchanges (14).

[16] Not least because of its role in fostering the spread of information about political decision-making through its bulletins and booklets: see, for example, European Bureau for Lesser Used Languages (1994).

Luxembourg, and Strasbourg, it becomes much more difficult for that country to deny the same right to its own constituent ethnic communities. But several other parts of the world have also seen positive political developments. The USA passed two Native American Languages Acts, in 1990 and 1992, the first 'to preserve, protect, and promote the rights of freedom of Native Americans to use, practice and develop Native American languages', the second 'to assist Native Americans in assuring the survival and continuing vitality of their languages'.[17] The 1991 Law on Languages of the Russian Federation gave all languages the status of a national property under the protection of the state. The 1991 Colombian Constitution gave indigenous languages official status in their own territories, and supported a bilingual education policy. On the wider world stage, UNESCO and the UN have produced various statements, such as the UN Declaration on the Rights of Persons belonging to National or Ethnic, Religious and Linguistic Minorities, adopted in 1992. Language, however, has tended to be just one of several cultural issues covered by these statements, hence the potential significance of the Universal Declaration of Linguistic Rights produced at Barcelona in 1996, with its primary focus on language (see Appendix). Statements, declarations, and resolutions are of course relatively easy to make; they are much harder to interpret in real social settings and to put into practice. The various formulations have all received their share of critical comment about the comprehensiveness of their coverage or the practicability of

---

[17] US Public Law 101–477; US Public Law 102–524.

their recommendations.[18] But they are certainly more specific and focused than earlier expressions of support for human rights, which have often not mentioned language at all, or done so in the vaguest of terms.

The need to maintain pressure on governments, at international, national, and local levels, to make sure that something is actually done, is therefore as critical as ever. Notwithstanding the above developments, there are probably still more countries in the world currently violating or ignoring language rights than supporting them. So there is no room for complacency. At the same time, the progress made in certain countries has to be acknowledged, as they provide illustrations of what can be done. Probably the most heart-warming case is in Paraguay, where Guaraní has come to be the chief sign of national identity, with official status (since 1992), enjoying widespread prestige, attracting great loyalty, and spoken by over 90% of the population. Paraguay was formerly considered to be a Spanish-speaking country in which Guaraní had a presence; today, some commentators reverse the description, talking about a Guaraní-speaking country in which Spanish has its place.[19] There has also been progress in Greenland, where Home Rule in 1979 led to a real increase in the numbers of bilingual Greenlanders appointed to senior positions.[20] And in Eritrea, as already noted, it is government policy to have no official language – an unusually liberal policy (especially in Africa: see p. 107) which was strongly affirmed by President Afewerki in 1995:[21]

[18] For some critical perspective, see the comments by Skutnabb-Kangas (1996: 8).
[19] For example, Rubin (1985).   [20] Langgaard (1992).
[21] Quoted by Brenzinger (1998: 94).

Our policy is clear and we cannot enter into bargaining. Everyone is free to learn in the language he or she prefers, and no one is going to be coerced into using this or that 'official' language.

4 An endangered language will progress if its speakers have a strong presence in the educational system

To promote a presence in the home is the priority, with any endangered language. As we have seen, it is no solution to develop a mindset which sees all the responsibility transferred to the school system.[22] But if there is no presence in the school system at all, at primary and secondary levels, the future is likewise bleak. The role of a school in developing a child's use of its mother tongue is now well understood, following several decades of research and debate in educational linguistics,[23] and while most of this work has been devoted to helping children improve their skills in unendangered languages, there is an immediate and obvious application to less fortunate linguistic situations. The school setting provides an increasingly widening range of opportunities for children to listen and speak, as they learn to cope with the demands of the curriculum and come to use the language in school-mediated social occasions (such as religious or cultural gatherings). It gives them the opportunity to engage with

[22] See above, p. 147. See also Fishman (1991).
[23] A useful synthesis of thinking, in relation to the UK's National Curriculum, is Brumfit (1995). See also Cantoni and Reyhner (1998) and Reyhner (1997).

literacy (see further below), which will open the doors to new worlds. If their only experience of speech and writing in school is through the medium of the dominant language, it will not be surprising to find that the indigenous language fails to thrive (an example of this happening was noted by Bradley in the case of the Ugong, above). Conversely, if careful planning has managed to give the indigenous language a formal place alongside the dominant language, the result can be a huge increase in the pupils' self-confidence.

Education is to some extent a mixed blessing, in endangered language situations. It introduces the pupils to the very foreign influences and values which have made their language endangered in the first place. At the same time, the knowledge and awareness which come from the process of education can generate a confidence which stands the children in good stead, as they find themselves coping with the difficulties of language maintenance. Knowing something about a language's history, folklore, and literature can be a great source of reassurance. The school is not the only source of this knowledge, of course. A great deal of language awareness, as well as social solidarity, results from the various forms of extra-curricular activity which a community can arrange as part of its language maintenance programme – for example, language playgroups, summer immersion camps, master-apprentice programmes, or bilingual holidays. And the same point applies in educational settings when older members of the community are involved. If 'educational system' is interpreted in its broadest sense, it will include all kinds of adult education courses in local halls and centres, community-based programmes, informal apprenticeships, in-service courses, and a great deal of activity that goes under the heading of 'awareness-raising'.[24]

But no teaching programme can succeed without good materials, and good materials are of no value unless there are teachers trained to use them. Teacher-training is thus a critical need, in most endangered situations. Ideally, these teachers would come from the population of fluent speakers left within the indigenous community, and their training would prepare them to cope with the non-speakers who will form the bulk of the next generation. The training required is complex, because the language-learning situation is so mixed. A great deal of the work is remedial, in the sense that many learners have varying levels of proficiency in the indigenous language, ranging from reasonable fluency to semilingualism. Many of the students will be members of the 'in-between' generation, who have learned the dominant language as a first language in order to assimilate, and who now have no alternative but to learn the ancestral language as if it were a foreign language. The teachers also have to cope with enormous variations in student temperament, ability, and motivation; a sociopolitical situation which may not always be sympathetic to their work; and an economic situation in which typically there is a shortage of materials and resources. The job, in short, is not easy, and demands proper status and pay – with indigenous teachers being paid comparably to visiting teachers who may have been imported to assist with the problem. Unfortunately, low

---

[24] For a useful distinction between 'language awareness' (working *on* what one knows) and 'consciousness-raising' (working *at* what one does not know), see James (1999).

salaries and discrepant levels are all too common, in endangered situations.

5 An endangered language will progress if its speakers can write their language down

The teaching of literacy is, of course, a major educational function; but literacy raises so many special issues that it requires a section to itself. It has a unique role in the maintenance of a language, as Samuel Johnson asserted, reflecting on the differences between a written and an unwritten language:[25]

Books are faithful repositories, which may be a while neglected or forgotten; but when they are opened again, will again impart their instruction: memory, once interrupted, is not to be recalled. Written learning is a fixed luminary, which, after the cloud that had hidden it has past away, is again bright in its proper station. Tradition is but a meteor, which, if once it falls, cannot be rekindled.

Just because a language is written down does not automatically mean it will survive, of course, as is evident from the many extinct languages of classical times which we know about only through their written records. But equally, once a language passes the stage where it can be transmitted between generations as the first language of the home, its future is vastly more assured if it can be written down. The reason is not simply to safeguard a corpus of data for posterity: if this were all that were

---

[25] 'Ostig in Sky', in *A journey to the Western Islands of Scotland*, p. 113 of the Penguin edition (Johnson 1990/1773).

required, these days it would be enough to make large numbers of audio or video recordings. The writing down of a language is a different kind of activity, as it involves an intellectual step – an analysis of the way the sound system of the language works, so that the most efficient form of spelling system can be devised, and the preparation of materials to aid learning, in the form of dictionaries, grammars, and other manuals. It is a step that linguists should be trained to do, in ways which will be reviewed below. It can also be a controversial step, so this postulate for progress needs to be viewed with caution.

For people whose culture has a history of several centuries of literacy, it can come as a surprise to realize that literacy has its downside, in relation to endangered languages. But there are several ways in which this can be so. To begin with, there may be resistance from the people themselves. If literacy has never been part of your culture, it is easy to see how its adoption could be perceived as a loss rather than a gain – a surrendering of that culture to a possibly hostile outside world, or a loss of ownership (see further below). Some people think of their language as being destroyed, once it is written down. And certainly, there is bound to be an effect on the way the language is represented: the stories of oral tradition are typically dynamic in character, varying between retellings, relying greatly on a lively interaction between speaker and listeners, and using an array of communicative effects of a non-verbal kind. When written down, they become static, reduced in form, and lacking a dialogic element; moreover, the alphabetical system is incapable of coping with the melodies, rhythms, tones of voice, gestures, and facial expressions that give the stories so much of their life. All recordings privilege one version above others; and in a tradition where the whole point is to allow for narrative variation, a great deal is lost as a consequence of the selection.

The decision to introduce literacy involves a second problem of selection. Which variety of the language shall be written down? Many endangered languages exist in a variety of dialects, some of which are very different from each other in sounds, grammar, and vocabulary. It is rarely possible, for reasons of practicality, to write them all down; so one dialect must be selected. What, then, happens to the others? Ironically, the very process of selection can be a factor leading to the loss of the diversity it was designed to safeguard.[26] A literacy programme tends to burn money, and resources which might otherwise have been used in support of a range of dialects suddenly turn out to be available no longer. Moreover, when a particular dialect is chosen for literacy, it inevitably acquires a higher status, and this can result in community divisiveness, which again might hasten the process of language loss. The problem is especially difficult in places where two different alphabetical systems are in competition, perhaps associated with different cultural or religious traditions – such as the Roman (Christian) and Arabic (Islamic). The decision to write down any of the unwritten endangered languages within the Arabic- or Hindi-speaking countries can lead to confrontations of this kind. It is easy to see why 'standardization is the single most technical issue in language reinforcement'[27] – needed

---

[26] For more on this viewpoint, see Mühlhausler (1995: 234; 1990).
[27] England (1998: 113).

before the production of written materials can make much progress.

It is important not to overstate the problems. Indeed, sometimes the risk is the opposite one – people become so positive about literacy that they develop a false sense of security, believing, for example, that once a language is written down it is thereby saved, and nothing more needs to be done. Literacy programmes have been successfully implemented in hundreds of endangered language situations, and are a priority in most revitalization projects.[28] Sometimes, two writing systems can be involved. In Yup'ik, for example, intergenerational transmission was at risk because the schoolchildren were having difficulty understanding the language of the elders. A book of elders' narratives was therefore compiled; and it was decided to print this in two orthographies. This was because the region was in a transition period between older missionary-developed orthographies which the elders would be used to, and the newer phonetic orthography which was being used in the schools. (This project had other interesting features. For instance, the compilers decided to keep the older, more difficult words in the text undefined, to encourage the children to ask their teachers, parents, and elders about them. This strategy shifted the emphasis away from the text and into the community, resulting in a more dynamic linguistic interaction.)[29]

---

[28] It is unclear just how many languages in the world have been written down. One estimate, using *Ethnologue* data, suggests 2,040 (about a third): see Trosterud (1999: 16).

[29] Wyman (1996: 20).

Even the question of competing dialects can be handled, with careful planning. An example is Quechua, where several local dialects were each given official status, all written in one alphabet.[30] Another is Romansh, where five dialects had each developed an individual literary norm. In 1978, a non-Romansh linguist, Heinrich Schmid, was given the task of devising a unified system which would treat each dialect impartially. The resulting 'Rumantsch Grischun' reflected the frequencies with which words and forms were used in the different dialects, choosing (when items were in competition) those which were most widespread. Although controversially received, as an artificial standard, it has since come to be increasingly used as a practical administrative tool, in official situations where the five dialects need a lingua franca. All dialects seem to have benefited from the newfound prestige, as a result.[31]

6 An endangered language will progress if its speakers can make use of electronic technology

To some extent, this is a hypothetical postulate, as many parts of the world where languages are most seriously

---

[30] Grinevald (1998: 130). However, the question of which way to represent standardized Quechua has proved contentious, as reported by Hornberger and King (1997: 19). One group supports an alphabet which has symbols for five vowels, showing Spanish colonial influence; another supports a system showing three vowels, which is more in line with the actual phonological structure of the language. The dispute has slowed the production of written materials, because publishers are naturally reluctant to invest in either system in case it is eventually rejected. Strongly held positions of this kind, though historically explicable, are a real hindrance to revitalization efforts, because they dissipate the energies of those who should be fighting on the same side.

[31] Haiman and Benincà (1992).

endangered have not yet come to benefit from electronic technology – or, for that matter, electricity. But in principle, information technology (IT) – and the Internet in particular – offers endangered languages which have been written down a fresh set of opportunities whose potential has hardly begun to be explored. The chief task presented by my first postulate above involved the need to give an endangered language a public profile. Traditionally, it is an expensive business: newspaper space, or radio and television time, does not come cheaply. Only the 'better-off' languages could afford to make routine use of these media. But with the Internet, everyone is equal. The cost of a Web page is the same, whether the contributor is writing in English, Spanish, Welsh, or Navajo. It is perfectly possible for a minority language culture to make its presence felt on the Internet, and this has begun to happen – notwithstanding the attempted repression of some languages by the occasional service-provider.[32] There are probably over 500 languages with an Internet presence now. What is significant, of course, is that the Net provides an identity which is no longer linked to a geographical location. People can maintain a linguistic identity with their relatives, friends, and colleagues, wherever they may be in the world. Whereas, traditionally, the geographical scattering of a community through migration has been an important factor in the dissolution of its language, in future this may no longer be the case. The Internet, along with the growth of faster and cheaper means of travel between locations, is altering our scenarios of endangerment.

---

[32] Recent reports include the closure of message boards in Irish by AOL (America OnLine) UK, reported in *Ogmios* 10. 23.

There is a great deal to be done before these scenarios become compelling. Software developers need to become more multilingual. More comprehensive coding conventions for non-Roman alphabets need to be implemented. And for many endangered communities, the basic possibility of an Internet connection is a long way off, given the lack of equipment – or even electricity. But there are already several signs of progress. A number of language maintenance projects have recruited language technologies to facilitate their task. For example, spelling-checkers have been used to help implement normalized spelling conventions in a newly written language – particularly useful where there is interference from some other language in the region. Computers have begun to handle bodies of specialized knowledge, such as lists of place names, genealogies, or plants. There has been a steady growth in computer-assisted self-study materials. One of the most promising signs is in the knowledge-management side of IT, where the importance of the notion of *localization* has steadily grown, to the extent that it must now be regarded as an industry in itself, with its own association, LISA (the Localization Industry Standards Association). In this context, *localization* refers to the adaptation of a product to suit a target language and culture, and is distinguished from both *globalization* (the adaptation of marketing strategies to regional requirements of all kinds) and *internationalization* (the engineering of a product, such as software, to enable efficient adaptation of the product to local requirements).[33] It is a healthy

---

[33] These definitions are from a report in *Language International* 10:4 (1998), 19. The report makes it clear that there is a great deal of variant usage over matters of definition throughout the industry.

sign to see this swing back from the global to the local, within such a short time, and it may be that endangered languages will be one of the domains which will benefit from this change of focus. At any rate, I am sufficiently convinced of the potential power of electronic technology to make it one of my six postulates for progress in language maintenance, notwithstanding the limited role it has been able to play in this domain hitherto.

My six postulates cut the cake in a certain way, and there are of course many other ways. Yet, despite differences of terminology and emphasis, similar themes recur. For example, Akira Yamamoto distinguishes nine factors 'that help maintain and promote the small languages':[34]

- the existence of a dominant culture in favour of linguistic diversity;
- a strong sense of ethnic identity within the endangered community;
- the promotion of educational programmes about the endangered language and culture;
- the creation of bilingual/bicultural school programmes;
- the training of native speakers as teachers;
- the involvement of the speech community as a whole;
- the creation of language materials that are easy to use;
- the development of written literature, both traditional and new;
- the creation and strengthening of the environments in which the language must be used.

And Lynn Landweer provides eight 'indicators of ethnolinguistic vitality' for an endangered language:[35]

---

[34] Yamamoto (1998b: 114).   [35] Landweer (1998).

- the extent to which it can resist influence by a dominant urban culture;
- the number of domains in which it is used;
- the frequency and type of code switching;
- the existence of a critical mass of fluent speakers;
- the distribution of speakers across social networks;
- the internal and external recognition of the group as a unique community;
- its relative prestige, compared with surrounding languages;
- its access to a stable economic base.

These lists have a great deal in common.

The role of the linguist

Linguists have been lurking in the background, in relation to each of these postulates, as indeed throughout earlier chapters, and it is time now to bring their role into the foreground. Or rather, roles – for there are several tasks of a specialized kind which have to be carried out in order to secure the future of a language. Adapting a metalanguage which has been well tried in clinical linguistics,[36] these tasks can be grouped into three broad types: those to do with diagnosis and assessment; those to do with description and analysis; and those to do with intervention and re-assessment.

The clinical analogy is particularly appropriate, as it enables us to take a stand about an issue which is raised

---

[36] See the discussion in Crystal (1981/1989). The medical analogy is also drawn by Valiquette (1998: 110).

from time to time: the linguist's motivation in working with endangered languages. My view is unequivocal: in exactly the same way as doctors only intervene with the primary aim of preserving the physiological health of patients, so linguists should only intervene with the primary aim of preserving the linguistic health of those who speak endangered languages. The concept of linguists working on such languages with no interest in the people who speak them – other than to see them as a source of data for a thesis or publication – is, or should be, as unacceptable a notion as it would be if doctors collected medical data without caring what happened subsequently to the patients. This point would not be worth making if it had not often happened. Indeed, it was once part of the research ethos. During the formative stages of linguistics, anthropology, and ethnography, data collection was routinely viewed as an end in itself. Once a corpus of data had been collected, it was treated as an autonomous entity, a contribution to a growing body of knowledge about human behaviour. In the case of linguistics, the aim was to increase the generality of descriptive statement and the power of theoretical explanation. It became so easy to forget about the people, while concentrating on the language. And the popular impression that scholars are preoccupied with their data while ignoring the problems of the real world surfaces regularly in relation to linguistics as it does elsewhere. Indeed, only a month before I wrote this paragraph I was involved in a radio discussion where one of the participants commented that dying languages 'must keep linguists very happy'. The point was made in a jocular tone, but its reiteration was uncomfortable, for it is a distraction from what the real issues are. The joke would not have been made about doctors. But then, linguists have never affirmed the equivalent of a Hippocratic oath. Perhaps they should.

None of this disallows linguists collecting data, analysing it, generalizing from it, speculating about it, and doing all the other things which do indeed keep them happy. That is what linguists are for – and we have to respect the interest which led them to become linguists in the first place. After all, there would be no linguists if we disregarded the needs of their own professional development, which chiefly involve the production of research publications and reference works. But in the field of endangered languages – as in the clinical field – this must not be the only motivation. Once linguists have decided to specialize in this area, they have to adopt a broader perspective, in which the aspirations of the indigenous community itself hold a central place. There has been much discussion about what this perspective should be. My own view is that linguists should see their broader role as helping an indigenous community understand what is unique about its linguistic heritage and what the forces are which threaten it. This means that one of their first tasks, under the general heading of diagnosis, is to grasp as much of the sociopolitical realities of endangered situations as they can. They need to appreciate the risks involved in stepping into a complex social setting, where to intervene in relation to one element may have unforeseen consequences elsewhere.[37] Language, it should be recalled from chapter 2, is just one element within an ecological system, and it is all too easy for linguists, even with the best of

---

[37] Thomas (1980: 90). See also chapter 3, fn. 9.

intentions, to harm the environment it was their hope to preserve. Even the initial selection of a language to study has political implications. There are always people around who will ask: why has one language been supported and not another? Once a language is chosen, there may be arguments about the support location: why work in town A and not in town B? The selection of consultants within the speech community (and their rates of pay) can also be contentious: why choose him and not her? It is easy for linguists, without realizing it, to find themselves apparently taking sides in a family feud, being aligned with a hidden political agenda, or being expected to fulfil a set of demanding social obligations. As Donna Gerdts has put it:[38]

Linguistic expertise is not sufficient for successful participation in a language program. The linguist must develop social and political skills to be an effective member of a language revitalization program.

Linguists who have worked a great deal with endangered languages – and here we have a further parallel with the clinical field – often remark on how emotionally stressful this sociopolitical context can be. Traditionally, there is nothing in a linguist's training which prepares for it. The concept of fieldwork commonly presented in courses is one where the methodological intricacies are well explained, but the psychological and social demands on the fieldworker are not. As experience grows, so this situation is slowly changing, especially in those academic departments where there is a strong commitment to

[38] Gerdts (1998: 13); the following quotation is from p. 21.

applied studies, and where the links with anthropology remain strong. But, as Gerdts wryly comments:

Young scholars should be warned … that, while endangered language research may seem like noble and interesting work, they will be faced with a hornet's nest of socio-political issues. The languages most in need of archiving are probably also the ones where the political situation is least hospitable. The good old days of popping in, doing some fieldwork, doing the analysis, going home, and publishing are gone forever.

There is still an enormous gap between the safe world of academic applied linguistics and the realities of endangered situations. The word 'safe' is not rhetoric: there are indeed physical dangers, given that many parts of the world are subject to crisis and conflict (see chapter 3), with irregular forces (terrorists or freedom fighters, depending on whose side you are on) and criminal operations posing an ever-present threat.[39] Rather more commonly, linguists find themselves faced with social and political obligations, simply by becoming a member, albeit a temporary one, of the indigenous community. The closeness of the bond varies greatly, but in small communities it can often amount to an intense commitment, even a familial responsibility. If an indigenous consultant falls ill, for example, the linguist may be called upon to help get the person to hospital. Moreover, in the Third World, a sense of the poverty of a region is never far away. There is a humanitarian need always in the

[39] It should not be forgotten, also, that there may be physical threat to the safety of the local consultants, as well as to the linguists. Not everyone in the indigenous community may be happy to see one of its members 'working with outsiders'.

background, which inevitably affects linguists (as human beings), and extends them in directions which go well beyond the strict needs of a linguistic enquiry (cf. p. 138). Several commentators have talked about the way linguists, as with aid workers, can become so mentally and physically exhausted by the pressure of the human need around them that they are unable to function professionally.

It has been called burnout.[40] They may also begin to question the value of their role, and be unable to control the ever-present doubt about whether they are really helping or just making things worse. There may, in addition, be hostility shown towards them by local people suspicious of their motives (especially if they are members of the society that threatened the community in the first place). Economic exploitation is so common that it is only natural for a community to assume that a Western investigator is there to make money out of them. And in the West itself, the suspicion may be there for political reasons, as Jens-Eberhard Jahn discovered in his work in Istria, Croatia, involving Croats, Slovenians, Italians, and others. Although he met some positive attitudes, he adds: 'I have also been accused of adding fuel to the fire of intolerance and ethnic hate by asking people about ethnic and linguistic attitudes', and he comments:[41]

This suspiciousness is an important factor to be reckoned with in researches of this kind: people who saw five different flags on their houses in the course of this century do not easily trust

---

[40] Rhydwen (1998: 104).
[41] Jahn (1998: 46, 47). For another example of linguistic research being seen as exploitation, see Yamamoto (1998a: 213).

anyone with a questionnaire asking about attitudes and language use, especially in the countryside and under ethnic minority conditions.

Not surprisingly, some fieldworkers give up. Fortunately, the vast majority do not. To begin with, by no means all endangered languages belong to such demanding parts of the world. But even in those locations where the task is difficult, it is perfectly possible to develop the required strengths and sensitivities. There are many linguists who have completed fieldwork projects or collaborated in language maintenance programmes that have been highly praised by indigenous communities and local government bodies. Confident in their linguistic professionalism, and experienced in the delicacies of sociopolitical situations, they have provided the right kind of advice and support at the right time, helping the community decide when something can usefully be done, and providing the expertise or training to enable them to do it. So often, it comes down to the question of deciding about priorities. In some places linguists may advise documentation of the language as rapidly as possible, because they have been able to perceive the true seriousness of the endangered situation. This was what one recent conference, on the situation in Africa, concluded.[42] In other places, the advice might be to get on with revitalization work as rapidly as possible, because an assessment of a local situation might indicate that there is a population ready to benefit from it. Both types of work involve multiple considerations.

---

[42] In a round-table discussion at the conference, Endangered Languages in Africa, held at Leipzig in 1997: see *Ogmios* 6. 22.

Documentation is a *sine qua non* of language maintenance. It is by no means the whole story, as we have seen – no language has ever been saved just by being documented – but an assessment of the documentation state of a language is an early priority in all investigations, and is a top priority in those cases where there is a real risk of impending language death. It is important to talk in terms of assessment, in all instances, because there are not enough opportunities and resources – or, for that matter, linguists – to waste effort on repeating what has been done already. We need to know what material may already exist within a community, or further afield, and what state it is in. Archive research is especially important in locations where early colonialists might have left materials – for example, there is an uncertain amount of material about South American languages in Spanish or Portuguese libraries, and there must be more in Italy, the Vatican, and elsewhere. If such material does exist, it needs to be preserved, and this may involve special technical measures, especially in cases where manuscripts are in a sensitive state. Devising secure repositories for material is in fact no small matter, especially in locations where rain, heat, and insects provide one kind of threat, theft provides another, collateral destruction by forces in a civil war provides a third, and the deliberate destruction of indigenous language materials by antagonistic governments provides a fourth.

What does documentation mean? We are not talking about the relatively straightforward task of gathering together a few words to act as symbols of heritage – such as we might see on souvenir mugs or in tourist magazines. Documentation is a major enterprise. Essentially we are talking about the permanent portrayal of a language using all available means. Face-to-face sessions with speakers, where utterances are systematically elicited and phonetically transcribed, are one method, enabling linguists to make immediate analytic decisions about sounds, patterns, and meanings which can then be checked directly with ethnic consultants. The language also has to be written down in a publicly usable alphabet. This can present a major technical problem (as well as the sociolinguistic problems referred to in the discussion of literacy above), especially in languages which have many sounds and tones; the Roman alphabet is inadequate, in most cases, and needs all kinds of letter combinations and diacritics to cope with the sometimes dozens of sounds not used in English. Much of the documentation effort, of course, will be devoted to the traditional tasks of compiling dictionaries and grammars;[43] but these days, a great deal of attention is also paid to the recording of patterns of discourse, in such genres as story-telling, prayers, and speech-making. Long word-lists and sets of grammatical paradigms go only a short way towards capturing what is

---

[43] The need for different kinds of dictionaries should be borne in mind. It is not just a matter of listing the words of the endangered language with a gloss in the linguist's language. Also desirable are dictionaries of the mutual influence between the endangered language and the other languages in the region with which it is in contact, especially the dominant language. The issue may be contentious (cf. chapter 4), but borrowings from the dominant language into the endangered language ought not to be excluded. Likewise, there may be scope for a dictionary of borrowings in the other direction – words that have been borrowed by the dominant language (e.g. Maori vocabulary in New Zealand English) – as this can add considerably to the prestige of the endangered language. The question of standardized spelling of course needs to have been resolved in such cases.

unique about a heritage; what is crucial is to show how the language is really used. Audio-recording facilities are especially important here, as they capture the dynamic aspects of the language (strategies of conversational interaction, for example) in ways that no other method can. Video facilities, if available, provide a record of the associated nonverbal communication, such as facial expression, gesture, and body posture and movement.

The *corpus* of a language comprises the set of (written, audio, video, multimedia) recordings which may have been made of it, along with all transcripts of speech, whether transcribed from tapes or from face-to-face interaction, and any other materials that are available, such as letters, place names, and historical documents. Only about 60% of the world's languages have had any kind of corpus compiled; and in many languages where some level of corpus work has been carried out, the material is often sporadic or biased (for example, related to the needs of Bible translation). Because in many cases it is this corpus which is going to be the only permanent record of a language, it is crucial that the quality and range of the data is as robust as possible. This means much more than ensuring that audio recordings are audible and clear (though that in itself can be difficult to guarantee). It means as far as possible obtaining material which is genuinely representative of the language and not a distortion of it (for example, not using someone with a speech defect). It means finding both male and female speakers, especially in languages where gender differences are systematically expressed in speech. It may also mean finding speakers of different ages, classes, professions, or kinship groups. People with specialized knowledge (for example, about animals, plants, or medicine) need to be paid special attention. Above all, in languages which are seriously endangered, it means finding people who are as fluent as possible, and who display as little as possible of the inconsistency and structural deterioration in the forms of the language which is so characteristic of obsolescence.[44] The level of competence of the consultants is obviously critical, given that the possibilities range from genuine fluency to a state in which there remain only fragmentary memories of a language. The possibility of fake data – invented forms presented by sharp informants who imagine the permanent presence of a linguist as a source of unending funds – also needs to be borne in mind.[45] But we have to be realistic: often, linguists have no options available to them. With last-speaker research, it is Hobson's choice.

Notwithstanding the need expressed above, to be sociopolitically aware, linguists must also respect the imperative (placed upon them in chapter 2, p. 71) to attend to the demands of their own subject, seen as a branch of human knowledge. They must respect the urgency of the intellectual need to document languages which, from a formal (as opposed to a sociolinguistic) point of view, are of especial importance to our understanding of the nature of language and its place in human history – particularly the way it can shed light on the nature of early civilization and the historical movement of peoples. Top priority in this context is the documentation

[44] For the state of the art in language obsolescence, see chapter 1, fn. 42.
[45] Some examples from Central America are referred to in Kaufman (1994: 34). The risk is everywhere.

of linguistic isolates – languages without a recognized affiliation – and of languages used in those parts of the world where linguistic relationships are uncertain. The north of Russia is one such area, where the languages are very diverse, and classification is controversial. South America is another important area because of its genetic diversity – it contains well over 100 families with about 70 of these being isolates – and here a great deal of basic documentation remains to be done. But every region has its isolates and its tentative proposals for family groupings; and even in those areas where work has begun, there is a great deal which needs to be done before these groupings reach the level of certainty found in Indo-European.

The size of the task is daunting, and requires a massive effort on the part of linguistics departments the world over.[46] It is an effort, moreover, which requires a fresh commitment, especially in those departments which have devoted the bulk of their intellectual and pedagogical energies to domains of linguistics which are at the opposite end of the scale from those required here. There is a growing concern, largely fuelled by the greater awareness of endangerment, that an important balance has been lost within linguistics – that the subject has become too 'theoretical' and insufficiently 'empirical'.[47] No one, I trust, is trying to set up the kind of false oppositions which were around half a century ago. The need for theoretical awareness on the empirical side is axiomatic.

---

[46] The cuts that have been made in schools and departments of languages in various parts of the world in recent years make the situation worse.

[47] For example, the point is made by Paul Newman and others in the Leipzig conference on Endangered Languages in Africa: see *Ogmios* 6. 20.

There have been excesses on that side too – notably the exclusive use of one analytical framework, tagmemics, in many parts of the world because of its favoured status as the approach used by the Summer Institute of Linguistics in its work in relation to Bible translation. But when we encounter training courses in linguistics which have given their students negligible amounts of phonetics exposure, or which omit courses on fieldwork and the associated anthropological/social perspectives required (to do with place names, personal names, genealogy, kinship, ethnobotany, etc.), it is plain – at least, to this writer – that we are a long way from having found the correct balance. Moreover, it must not be forgotten that a significant part of the encounter with endangered languages is in relation to intervention, and this puts the field of preventive linguistics (as I have been calling it) firmly within the domain of applied linguistics – another area which has been treated dismissively by some academic linguistics departments. Indeed, some of the recognized fields within applied linguistics are of considerable relevance to the work, such as foreign language teaching, language learning, error analysis, and lexicography. Nor is an outline perspective enough. When we are dealing with a situation where the only source of data for a language is one person's transcription, it is critical for that person to have the best possible phonetics training. When we are dealing with such sensitive sociopolitical situations as those described above, a thorough grounding in fieldwork principles and practice is obligatory. And the theoretical and methodological issues involved in preventive linguistics are certainly no less critical than those involved in such fields as clinical linguistics.

The revitalization team

Languages need communities in order to live. So, only a community can save an endangered language. This point is fundamental:[48]

The community, and only the community, can preserve a living language. If the community surrenders its responsibility to outsiders, or even to a few persons within the community (such as school teachers), the language will die. Language preservation efforts must involve the total community, and not just a part of it.

The saving of a language demands commitment, a shared sense of responsibility, a clear sense of direction, and a wide range of special skills. 'Many languages need management to survive.'[49] That is why, in many parts of the world, we see the emergence of a team approach to language maintenance – recognition of the fact that the task is so great that it needs proper planning and management, and the involvement of selected people with individual skills, acting on behalf of the community as a whole. While situations vary widely, there are a number of steps which have to be taken (though the following order is in no way obligatory):[50]

- community members and outside fieldworkers meet, get to know each other, and form a working team;
- the nature of the problem needs to be agreed – that the language is indeed endangered, that it is the

---

[48] Valiquette (1998: 107).   [49] Wurm (1991: 3).

[50] The list is a synthesis and expansion of recommendations made by various people: see, in particular, Yamamoto (1998b: 118), Valiquette (1998: 109–10), England (1998: 106).

responsibility of the community to do something about it, and that something can be done about it;

- the local situation is given a general assessment, taking into account the sociopolitical or religious sensitivities to be respected, and other issues to do with authenticity, standardization, ownership, and control;
- a survey of language use is carried out, to decide whether there are urgent short-term tasks to be carried out, and whether the long-term focus needs to be on first language learning, second language teaching, or both;
- the kind of preservation has to be decided, the possibilities ranging from the provision of a symbolic heritage presence within a dominant culture to a full-scale independent presence as a daily spoken and written medium;
- the nature and extent of the commitment by team members is explored, in relation to both long-term and short-term planning;
- immediate objectives are established, including the balance of activity to be devoted to recording, documentation, teaching, the writing of materials, and so on;
- procedures for data collection and storage are agreed;
- 'model' speakers of the language are identified and enlisted as consultants;
- data collection is carried out;
- analysis of the data is undertaken, with the aim of producing an account of the language's structure, in the form of a grammar and dictionary, etc.;
- a process of standardization is introduced, for both speech and writing, and a publicly usable alphabet devised;

- strategies are introduced for reinforcing the use of the language in homes and other domestic settings;
- strategies are introduced for expanding the use of the written language in the public domain;
- strategies are introduced for expanding the use of the spoken language in the public domain;
- strategies are introduced for giving the language a presence in schools, with the aim of making it a medium of instruction;
- curriculum materials are written and published, for both child and adult use;
- texts in the language, of general public interest (such as stories, poems, newspaper articles), are written and published;
- principles need to be established to get the language recognized as an official regional language.

It can be seen from this list that revitalization teams need several types of person to be most effective – ideally community administrators, elders, good general speakers and speakers with specialized knowledge, teachers, materials designers and writers, and linguists. In a truly ideal world, the community itself would have members who could fulfil all these roles; in practice, outside help is usually required for the linguistic side of the work, and often for the teaching and materials side too.

However, reports from fieldworkers in several places indicate that the concept of a 'team', with all the positive resonances we associate with that term, is often not an easy goal to achieve, partly because of the different agendas being followed by communities and linguists (as discussed earlier in this chapter), and partly because of a lack of mutual understanding about their different roles. As the initiative is generally coming from outside, the onus is on the linguist to understand what local communities want. According to Donna Gerdts, there are three main issues: they want their language and culture back; they want control of all aspects of education and research; and they want autonomy – the opportunity to do the work themselves without foreign experts.[51] If this is so, then the primary aim of intervention on the part of the outside linguist must be to train local people in the linguistic skills required – insofar as there are possible candidates available. Not only must the work be *'on* a language, *for* its speakers and *with* its speakers',[52] it also needs to be *'by* its speakers'. There is no conflict here with the urgency of the linguistic need for documentation, as it is precisely by working through the processes involved in this task that training is carried out. One learns by doing – a well-established routine in other domains of applied linguistics.

Some of the issues in the above listing are highly complex, and require considerable discussion at an early stage. For example, the question of ownership, already introduced in chapter 3, raises many sensitive issues. In some cultures, to begin with, not everyone is entitled to recite a

---

[51] Gerdts (1998: 17).
[52] Grinewald (1998: 156). The same point is made by Yamamoto (1998b: 118). See also Furbee, Stanley, and Arkeketa (1998: 79): 'It is the job of the outside consultant to help the tribe find such people [to become language scholars], train them, and step aside.' For examples of teacher-training programmes, see the American Indian Language Development Institutes in Arizona and Oklahoma described in Yamamoto (1998b: 115).

particular story, or sing a particular song. There is a recognized notion of ownership, often depending on kinship within a clan, or a person's age, or someone's status within ceremonial protocol.[53] Losing control of a particular use of language – for example, by tape-recording it or writing it down – is therefore viewed as a very serious matter. There may be a genuine fear that ethnic materials will be exploited by people who do not understand them – becoming the butt of jokes, or distorted through stereotypes in film and television, or desecrated by being retold in inappropriate settings. Writing the language down may be seen as a dilution of the 'real' language, which is spoken (cf. above). Some elders therefore do not want to tell their stories; and even if they do, their relatives or community groups may dispute their right to tell them, or refuse to allow other people to use them. The ancestral language may be viewed as sacred. Arguments can be bitter, and linguists have reported instances where people have stopped recording sessions taking place, and where tapes already recorded have been sabotaged. In the worst-case scenario, the issue has become so contentious, with members of a community taking different sides, that access to a body of recordings is denied to everyone. The tapes or transcripts are kept locked away.

Linguists obviously have great difficulty operating in such circumstances. All they can do is draw attention to the consequences of such actions – that there will come a time when no one will be left to interpret what is in the recordings (assuming the tapes have physically survived),

[53] This notion of ownership is explored in Dauenhauer and Dauenhauer (1998: 91ff.).

and that the next generation will not be able to understand them. The core argument is that the concept of *ownership* of a language needs to be balanced with that of *stewardship*. Linguists can also suggest practical solutions – ways in which ownership can be made manifest for posterity. The name, picture, and biography of an oral performer, or an appropriate set of clan symbols and commentary, can become a formal part of the procedure. This kind of thing is often done with indigenous paintings and crafts; it can be a routine part of language 'products' too. When the options are pointed out, and if the issue is handled sensitively, people can be persuaded; indeed, they can take great pride in the language materials which they originated, as can the whole community. When this happens, the prognosis for the future of the language is improving.

There is another concept of ownership which needs to be considered – the issue of intellectual property rights. According to Donna Gerdts, this is the issue which most often delays or halts the progress of a project.[54] The local community may view the linguistic work as yet another attempt to 'steal' their language, or as an opportunity for outsiders to profit from it, and they therefore claim ownership of the data which linguists record or transcribe, and the analyses and materials they make. Linguists working alone in these situations, on the other hand, having put in so much time and expertise to produce these results, and without whom there would *be* no results, also claim some rights in the matter. Conflicts over the rights to data and dissemination have evidently led to frequent major

---

[54] Gerdts (1998: 19–21).

breakdowns in the collaborative process between local community and visiting linguist, amounting at times to litigation. Perhaps the worst of the 'horror stories' (Gerdts) are a consequence of the stage of development of preventive linguistics, which is still working out a concept of best practice. In principle, the issues are no different from those already encountered in literary or clinical work, where scrupulous attention must be devoted to issues of data gathering, permissions to reproduce data, and data dissemination, before linguistic analysis can proceed. Ultimately, copyright of the raw data must remain with the community, just as copyright of literary data remains with the author. However, the situation with indigenous languages is inevitably more complex, in that there is usually no tradition of understanding to rely upon (as in the concept of 'fair quotation' in publishing) and often no clear legal notion of copyright – a notion which is in any case of Western origin. Research agreements therefore have to be made at the outset of any project, and decisions made about the distribution of responsibilities, costs, and profits (e.g. royalties).

If a positive approach to teamwork can be quickly achieved, the study of endangered languages gains immensely, and everything seems achievable. The same effect has been noted in clinical and educational linguistics, where teamwork is also critical for success. Everything depends on a recognition of individual strengths and limitations. There are certain things which linguists cannot do, and where they are wholly dependent on other members of the team. For example, linguists are not the ones to instil a sense of enthusiasm within a community on behalf of a language; nor are they able to function as teachers of culture, nor – in most cases – as fluent teachers of the endangered language. Most linguists are not even able to be full time within a community, as they hold jobs elsewhere and are available only at certain times of the year. On the other hand, linguists have experience which other members of the team do not have. Apart from the more obvious skills in language transcription and analysis, or in writing up results for archiving or publication, they usually have more awareness than other people of how funding can be obtained or maintained – for example, they will be more used to writing grant applications, or keeping records of project targets for funding organizations. They will be more used to speaking in public, and can thus act as mediators between the community and political or educational bodies – such as by presenting a case on behalf of the community in a government enquiry, or translating legal documents relating to civil or language rights. They may even find themselves in court, providing evidence in support of the community in a land claim or other issue of social justice. The study of place names, or tribal genealogies, for example, may be critical in deciding the boundaries of a treaty or the extent of its application. In such cases, though the role of the linguist is restricted in scope, it can be critical.

The success of a team approach depends very much on its members having an accurate and realistic awareness of the contribution which each can make to the project. Community members of the team need to be clear about what the abilities of linguists actually are. They must not expect linguists to be polyglots (the other sense of 'linguist') or to have native-speaker fluency in their language. Linguists have often found themselves being criticized for 'having an accent' or 'making errors' by local people who have not grasped the nature of the analytical role which linguists perform. The complexity of the task of phonetic transcription is also usually underestimated, as well as that of developing a new writing system. Moreover, the members of an indigenous community, once involved, are anxious for quick results, and can become impatient or disillusioned when these are not forthcoming. While linguists can do a lot, they are not magicians, and if the data sources are weak, or time is short, or conditions are poor, there is a limit to what can be done.

Linguists, correspondingly, need to develop their sense of what the community members of the team require, and respond positively when requests are put to them for help. They may end up performing all kinds of activities which they would not normally do, or which they would consider to be linguistically unimportant. For example, they may be asked to produce simple lists of words and phrases in response to a particular local need (such as a tourist leaflet), or to provide captions or labels for a museum exhibition. Such tasks might have little or no linguistic significance, as far as the discovery of new facts about the language is concerned, but they can be of considerable social value, in the eyes of the community. Linguists may also find themselves being asked to spend precious time producing versions of their findings which are accessible to non-specialists – a point which becomes critical when dealing with the provision of teaching materials. They also need to appreciate that the community may want to be kept informed about what they are doing, even though they might not be happy about making public a set of findings which they consider to be preliminary and tentative. In the final analysis, as Donna Gerdts asserts, it is the community which is in charge:[55]

A linguist working on an endangered language must submit to the authority of the community administrators. At every turn, the linguist will have to compromise long-range scholarly goals to meet the community's immediate needs.

But the gap between the two viewpoints is still very great. As Colette Grinevald puts it:[56]

Bridging the gap between academic linguistics and community wants and efforts is surely one of the major challenges of the linguistic profession as it faces the situation of endangered languages at the turn of the new century.

None of this thinking is unique to working with endangered languages. Every point just made I have encountered before in relation to language pathology.

But there is one point of difference, when we compare clinical and preventive linguistics. Following the death of a language-disordered person, the story is over. But following the death of a language, the story may not be over, for people at some point may wish to resurrect it. Indeed, this possibility is very real in the minds of linguists, as they try to document dying languages: one day a community may wish to make contact with its interrupted linguistic heritage, and reintroduce the ancestral language into its community – insofar as it can be reconstructed from available resources. Can dead languages be revived in this way? And, if such efforts are made, might not a Frankenstein's monster of a language be the result?

[55] Gerdts (1998: 21).   [56] Grinevald (1998: 143).

In fact, limited success has been achieved in several instances, and with opportunities now to record dying languages using audio and video facilities, the situation can only improve. The classic case of language revival is, of course, Hebrew – though this is a contentious example, as we saw above (p. 169), because of the question of just how much continuity there has been in the use of the language in the Jewish diaspora since Classical times. Stephen Wurm reports an uncontentious instance: the case of Kaurna, an Aboriginal language of South Australia.[57] This language had been extinct for about a century, but had been quite well documented; so, when a strong movement grew for its revival, progress was possible. The revived language is not the same as the original language, of course; most obviously, it lacks the breadth of functions which it originally had, and large amounts of old vocabulary are missing. But, as it continues in present-day use, it will develop new functions and new vocabulary, just as any other living language would, and as long as people value it as a true marker of their identity, and are prepared to keep using it, there is no reason to think of it as anything other than a valid system of communication. This is not the only Australian case, according to Wurm; and several other instances have been noted elsewhere. Britain has seen the re-emergence of Cornish in Cornwall after an appreciable interval, and efforts are underway to make progress with Manx in the Isle of Man. It is too soon to predict the future of these revived languages, but they do exist, and are in some parts of the world attracting precisely the range of positive attitudes and grass-roots

[57] Wurm (1998: 193).

215

support which are the preconditions for language survival. In such unexpected but heart-warming ways might we see the grand total of languages in the world minimally increased.

Conclusions

Language death is a terrible loss, to all who come into contact with it: 'Facing the loss of language or culture involves the same stages of grief that one experiences in the process of death and dying.'[58] We do not have to be members of an endangered community to sense this grief, or respond to it. Anyone who has worked with these communities, even over a short period, knows that it is a genuine insight, well justifying the dramatic nature of the analogy. And it is this keen, shared sense of loss which fuels the motivation and commitment of linguists, community groups, and support organizations in many parts of the world.

The growth in linguistic awareness about the problem, and the emergence of an associated activism, was one of the most exciting developments of the 1990s. Although awareness is still poor among the general public, the issues are now being much more widely discussed at professional levels, in a variety of international, national, regional, and local contexts. At one extreme, there are major campaigns such as those involved in promulgating the Barcelona Declaration of Linguistic Rights, or such initiatives as the 'Red Book on Endangered Languages' (part of the Tokyo Clearing House project: see Appendix).

[58] Dauenhauer and Dauenhauer (1998: 71).

What can be done?

At the other extreme, there is lively debate taking place within many of the endangered communities themselves. Mechanisms and structures are now in place to channel energies. Short-, medium-, and long-term aims are now much clearer, as a result of the conferences and publications of the 1990s – many of which I have relied upon in this book. Preventive linguistics, as a subject, is still very largely at the stage of case studies, building up an empirical database to act as a testing ground for the hypotheses about the causes, processes, and consequences of language death. But it is a subject which is showing signs of real growth.

How far it will grow is currently unclear. It depends, to some extent, on a maturation of attitude towards research into endangered languages from within the profession of linguistics itself. The harsh realities of working in endangered situations have often not been appreciated by linguists used to working only with healthy languages. Experienced fieldworkers have often emphasized that old speakers or last speakers can be hard to find and hard to work with. Moreover, such consultants are not all orators: sometimes they say very little, and what they do say may be full of inconsistencies. It may take a lot of time and money to obtain a small amount of data, whose range and quality may fall well short of what is usually found in academic studies, such as a thesis or journal publication. There may be no point of major theoretical import to be discovered. By all accounts, some of those with seniority in the linguistics profession, who accept students for research or who evaluate journal articles, are still some way from understanding this. I therefore applaud the clear stance taken by the Linguistic Society of America,

217

in a 1994 policy statement, which recommended that linguistics departments should 'support the documentation and analysis of the full diversity of the languages which survive in the world today, with highest priority given to the many languages which are closest to becoming extinct, and also to those languages which represent the greatest diversity', recognizing that the collection and analysis of such data is 'a fundamental and permanent contribution to the foundation of linguistics', and urging that the value of the work should be recognized 'through the awarding of advanced degrees and through favorable hiring, promotion, and/or tenure decisions'.[59]

Growth also depends on imponderables, such as the emergence of fresh international trends. It is difficult to predict the consequences of new supranational political and economic entities, such as the European Union or the various Free Trade Associations. One likely effect is a stronger reassertion of local regional identities, and with this will come greater political support for minority groups, and the possibility of funding. For ultimately, growth in this domain depends, fundamentally, on the availability of funding. There are several people willing to 'get out there', but the shortage of money means that only a tiny number of projects can be supported. This is the message, repeatedly, from the organizations which are trying to raise funds. For example, the Endangered Language Fund in its second year managed to support 10 projects – but out of a field of 70 applicants, and mostly at a lower level than was requested; there was a similar story

---

[59] Committee on Endangered Languages and their Preservation (1994: 5).

from the Foundation for Endangered Languages, which in 1998 managed to contribute to 4 projects out of 30.[60] Much of the focus, moreover, has so far been short-term. There is an urgent need for projects which devote their energies to long-term planning, in relation to intervention. After all, we are dealing with a problem whose effects can be alleviated, but certainly not solved, in the short term. The point is readily illustrated from those programmes which have been active for many years – 25 years, in the case of Mohawk, to take just one example.[61] The question of what works and why, when engaging in revitalization, is the really difficult one, just as it is in clinical interventions. The question can be answered, but it requires longitudinal research, and this takes several years, and is always expensive.

The present generation is the first to have enough data available to be able to make a true assessment of the situation. Having made it, the outcome, as we have seen, is bleak. Faced with the likelihood of losing half the world's languages within the next century, and of the distinct possibility of a world with only one language in it a few hundred years hence, it is this generation which

---

[60] See The *Endangered Language Fund Newsletter* 2:2 (1998), 1–4. For an account of other early grants from this Fund, see *Ogmios* 6 (1997), 16–17; and for the first grants from the Foundation for Endangered Languages, see *Ogmios* 7 (1998), 3; *Ogmios* 10 (1998), 3–4. The situation is not helped by uncertainty in the world's currency markets: devaluation of a local currency can have a devastating effect on a revitalization project – as reported, for example, by a Nahuatl publishing project in 1996: see *Iatiku* 2 (1996), 7.

[61] Jacobs (1998: 122). To document a language and provide the basis for its maintenance takes 'upward of 20 years', according to SIL linguist Lynn Landweer (1998: 64).

needs to make the decisions. We have two choices. We can sit back and do nothing, and let things just wind down. Already a great deal of time has elapsed since linguists began to get their act together, and Nancy Dorian makes the point:[62]

Having waited too long before undertaking to rally support for threatened languages, we may find ourselves eulogizing extinct languages whose living uniqueness we had hoped instead to celebrate.

The alternative is to act, using as many means as possible to confront the situation and influence the outcome. We know that intervention can be successful. Revitalization schemes can work. But time is running out. It is already too late for many languages, but we hold the future of many others in our hands. The linguists in the front line, who are actually doing the fieldwork, therefore need as much support as we can mobilize. The raising of public awareness is a crucial step, and this book I hope will play its part in that task.

The urgency of the need to get things done has no parallel elsewhere within linguistics. Languages are dying at an unprecedented rate. If the estimates I reviewed in chapter 1 are right, another six or so have gone since I started to write this book.

[62] Dorian (1998: 21).

APPENDIX

Some relevant organizations

~

This list contains all the organizations mentioned in the body of this book, plus a selection of other points of contact around the world.

Ad Hoc Committee on Endangered Languages
c/o Université de Québec à Montréal, CP 8888, succ. Centre-ville, Montréal, Québec H3C 3P8, Canada.
M366050@er.uqam.ca

Committee on Endangered Languages and their Preservation (CLEP)
c/o Linguistic Society of America, 1325 18th Street, NW, Washington DC 20036–6501
lsa@lsadc.org

The Endangered Language Fund, Inc
c/o Doug Whalen, Department of Linguistics, Yale University, New Haven, CT 06520, USA
whalen@haskins.yale.edu
http://sapir.ling.yale.edu/~elf/study.html

Endangered-Languages-L Electronic Forum
c/o: Mari Rhydwen, Graduate School of Education, University of Western Australia, Nedlands, Perth, WA 6009, Australia
majordomo@coombs.anu.edu.au
mrhydwen@decel.ecel.uwa.edu.au

Ethnologue
c/o Barbara Grimes, Summer Institute of Linguistics Inc,
International Linguistics Center, 7500 West Camp
Wisdom Road, Dallas, TX 75236, USA
http://www.sil.org/ethnologue

European Bureau of Lesser Used Languages
c/o Information Centre, rue Saint-Josse 49B / Sint-
Jooststraat 49B, 1030 Brussels
fax: (+32 2) 2181974

The Foundation for Endangered Languages
c/o Nicholas Ostler, Batheaston Villa, 172 Bailbrook
Lane, Bath BA1 7AA.
nostler@chibcha.demon.co.uk
http://www.bris.ac.uk/Depts/Philosophy/CTLL/FEL

Gesellschaft für bedrohte Sprachen (Society for
Endangered Languages)
c/o Hans-Jürgen Sasse, Institut für Sprachwissenschaft,
Universität zu Köln, 50923 Köln, Germany
GBS@uni-koeln.de/phil-fak/ifs/pages/d_agbs.htm

**Institute for the Preservation of the Original
Languages of the Americas**
c/o Executive Director, 713 1/2A Canyon Road, Santa Fe,
New Mexico 87501, USA
ipola@roadrunner.com

**International Clearing House for Endangered
Languages (ICHEL)**
c/o Kazuto Matsumura, Department of Asian and Pacific
Linguistics, Institute of Cross-Cultural Studies, University of Tokyo, Hongo 7–3–1, Bunkyo-ku, Tokyo 113,
Japan
kmatsum@tooyoo.L.u-tokyo.ac.jp
http://www.tooyoo.L.u-tokyo.ac.jp

Language Documentation Urgency List
c/o Dietmar Zaefferer, Institut für Deutsche Philologie,
Universität München, Schellingstr. 3, D-80799, München,
Germany
ue303bh@sunmail.lrz-muenchen.de

List Endangered-Languages-L
http://carmen.murdoch.edu.au/lists/endangered-languages-
l/ell-websites.html

Logosphere
c/o David Dalby, Observatoire Linguistique, Hebron,
Dyfed SA34 0XT, UK
logosphere@aol.com

Network on Endangered Languages
c/o T. Matthew Ciolek, Computer Centre, Research
School of Pacific and Asian Studies, Australian National
University, Canberra, Australia
coombspapers@coombs.anu.edu.au

**Society for the Study of the Indigenous Languages of
the Americas**
c/o Victor Golla, Department of Native American Studies,
Humboldt State University, Arcata, CA 95521.
gollav@axe.humboldt.edu

**Terralingua: Partnerships for Linguistic and Biological
Diversity**
c/o David Harmon, PO Box 122, Hancock, Michigan
49930–0122, USA
http://cougar.ucdavis.edu/nas/terralin/home.html

UNESCO (Study of Endangered Languages)
c/o Jean Biengen, Secretary-General, CIPSH (International Council for Philosophy and Humanistic Studies),
1 rue Miollis, 75732 Paris, France
fax: 33–1–406559480

UNESCO (World Languages Report)
c/o Paul Ortega, UNESCO Centre Basque Country,
Alameda de Urquijo, 60, ppal. Dcha, E-48011 Bilbao, País
Vasco (Spain)
http://www.unescoeh.org
unescopv@eurosur.org

Universal Declaration of Linguistic Rights
c/o Follow-up Committee, Rocafort 242 bis 2n, =20,
08029 Barcelona, Catalunya, Spain
dudl@linguistic-declaration.org
http://www.linguistic-declaration.org

REFERENCES

Adams, Douglas. 1979. *The hitch-hiker's guide to the galaxy.* London: Pan.

Adelaar, William F. H. 1998. The endangered situation of native languages in South America. In Matsumura (ed.), 1–15.

Ahlers, Jocelyn, and Leanne Hinton. 1997. Authenticity in the context of California native languages. *Foundation for Endangered Languages Newsletter* 5. 18–19.

Aitchison, Joan. 1991. *Language change: progress or decay?* 2nd edn. Cambridge: Cambridge University Press.

Andersen, Ole Stig. 1998. The burial of Ubykh. In Abstracts for the Open Forum, supplement to Ostler (ed.), 3.

Annamalai, E. 1998. Language survival in India: challenges and responses. In Matsumura (ed.), 17–31.

Arcand, Jean-Louis. 1996. Development economics and language: the earnest search for a mirage? *International Journal of the Sociology of Language* 121. 119–57.

Atwood, Margaret. 1995. Marsh languages. In *Morning in the burned house.* Boston: Houghton Mifflin; reprinted in *Ogmios* 8 (1998), 28.

Babe, R. E. 1997. Understanding the cultural ecology model. In Cliché (ed.), 1–23.

Baker, Colin, and Sylvia Prys Jones. 1998. *Encyclopedia of bilingualism and bilingual education.* Clevedon: Multilingual Matters.

Ball, Martin J., ed. 1988. *The use of Welsh.* Clevedon: Multilingual Matters.

Bamford, Samuel. 1854. *The dialect of South Lancashire.* London: John Russell Smith.

Bamgbose, Ayo. 1997. Contribution to the symposium on Endangered Languages in Africa, Leipzig. *Ogmios* 6. 21–2.

Barnes, J. 1984. Evidentials in the Tuyuca verb. *International Journal of American Linguistics* 50. 255–71.

Barthes, Roland. 1977. Déclaration. In *Fragments d'un discours amoureux*. Paris: Editions du Seuil.

Bauer, Laurie, and Peter Trudgill, eds. 1998. *Language myths*. Harmondsworth: Penguin.

Bauman, James A. 1980. *A guide to issues in Indian language retention*. Washington: Center for Applied Linguistics.

Bauman, Richard, and Joel Sherzer, eds. 1974. *Explorations in the ethnography of speaking*. Cambridge: Cambridge University Press.

Bellin, Wynford. 1984. Welsh and English in Wales. In Peter Trudgill (ed.), *Language in the British Isles*. Cambridge: Cambridge University Press, 449–79.

Benton, Richard A. 1996. Language policy in New Zealand: defining the ineffable. In Michael Herriman and Barbara Burnaby (eds.), *Language policies in English-dominant countries*. Clevedon: Multilingual Matters, 62–98.

Bergsland, Knut. 1998. Two cases of language endangerment: Aleut and Sámi. In Matsumura (ed.), 33–48.

Bernard, H. Russell. 1992. Preserving language diversity. *Human Organization* 51. 82–9.

Bixler, M. T. 1992. *Winds of freedom: the story of the Navajo code talkers of World War II*. Darien, CT: Two Bytes.

Blench, Roger. 1998. Recent fieldwork in Nigeria: report on Horom and Tapshin. *Ogmios* 9. 10–11.

Bloch, Bernard, and George Trager. 1942. *Outline of linguistic analysis*. Baltimore: Linguistic Society of America.

Bloomfield, Leonard. 1933. *Language*. London: Allen and Unwin.

Bodmer, Frederick. 1944. *The loom of language*. London: Allen and Unwin.

Borst, Arno. 1957–63. *Der Turmbau von Babel*, 6 vols. Stuttgart: Hiersemann.

Boswell, James. 1785. *The journal of a tour to the Hebrides*. London: Charles Dilly.

1791. *The life of Samuel Johnson*. London: Charles Dilly.

Bourhis, R., H. Giles, and H. Tajfel. 1974. Language as a determinant of Welsh identity. *European Journal of Social Psychology* 3. 447–60.

Bradley, David. 1989. The disappearance of Ugong in Thailand. In Dorian (ed.), 33–40.

1998. Minority language policy and endangered languages in China and Southeast Asia. In Matsumura (ed.), 49–83.

Brenzinger, Matthias. 1995. Contribution to a seminar on Endangered Languages at Dartmouth College, Hanover (New Hampshire, USA). *Iatiku* 1. 5.

1998. Various ways of dying and different kinds of deaths: scholarly approaches to language endangerment on the African continent. In Matsumura (ed.), 85–100.

Brenzinger, Matthias, Bernd Heine, and Gabriele Somner. 1991. Language death in Africa. In Robins and Uhlenbeck (eds.), 19–44.

Bright, William, ed. 1992. *The international encyclopedia of linguistics*. Oxford and New York: Oxford University Press.

Brumfit, Christopher, ed. 1995. *Language education in the National Curriculum*. Oxford: Blackwell.

Bullock, A., O. Stallybrass, and S. Trombley, eds. 1988. *The Fontana dictionary of modern thought*. 2nd edn. London: Fontana.

Cantoni, Gina, and Jon Reyhner. 1998. What educators can do to aid community efforts at indigenous language revitalization. In Ostler (ed.), 33–7.

Carroll, J. B., ed. 1956. *Language, thought and reality*. Cambridge, MA: MIT Press.

Chafe, W., and J. Nichols, eds. 1986. *Evidentiality: the linguistic coding of epistemology*. Norwood, NJ: Ablex.

Chambers, J. K., and P. Trudgill. 1980. *Dialectology*. Cambridge: Cambridge University Press.

Champion, S. G., ed. 1938. *Racial proverbs*. London: Routledge.

Chomsky, A. N. 1957. *Syntactic structures*. The Hague: Mouton.

Cliché, Danielle, ed. 1997. *Cultural ecology: the changing dynamics of communications*. London: International Institute of Communications.

Committee on Endangered Languages and their Preservation. 1994. The need for the documentation of linguistic diversity. *Linguistic Society of America Bulletin* 144 (June 1994). 5.

Connell, Bruce. 1997. Kasabe (Luo). *Iatiku* 4. 27.

Coulmas, Florian. 1992. *Language and economy*. Oxford: Blackwell.

Craig, Colette. 1992. A constitutional response to language endangerment: the case of Nicaragua. *Language* 68. 17–24.

Crow, Ron. 1997. Guest editorial in *Iatiku* 4. 3–4.

Crystal, David. 1981/9. *Clinical linguistics*. Vienna: Springer / London: Whurr.

　　1982. Terms, time and teeth. *British Journal of Disorders of Communication*, 17. 3–19.

　　1985. *Linguistics*. 2nd edn. Harmondsworth: Penguin.

　　1997a. *Cambridge encyclopedia of language*. 2nd edn. Cambridge: Cambridge University Press.

　　1997b. *English as a global language*. Cambridge: Cambridge University Press.

　　ed. 1997c. *The Cambridge encyclopedia*. 3rd edn. Cambridge: Cambridge University Press.

　　1998. Moving towards an English family of languages? In O. Alexandrova and M. Konurbayev (eds.), *Folia Anglistica* (Festschrift for Olga S. Akhmanova on 'World Englishes'). Moscow: Moscow State University, 84–95.

　　1999. 'From out in left field? That's not cricket.' Finding a focus for the language curriculum. In R. S. Wheeler (ed.), *The workings of language*. New York: Praeger.

Dalby, David. 1997. Exploring the Logosphere: review of results. Paper presented at the Logosphere Workshop, School of Oriental and African Studies, London, 11 September 1997.

Daniszewski, John. 1997. Teacher tries to rescue language spoken by Jesus. *Los Angeles Times*, 29 March 1997, A1.

Dante. *c.* 1304. *De vulgari eloquentia*, translated by A. G. Ferrers Howell.

Dauenhauer, Nora Marks, and Richard Dauenhauer. 1998. Technical, emotional, and ideological issues in reversing language shift: examples from Southeast Alaska. In Grenoble and Whaley (eds.), 57–98.

Dimmendaal, Gerrit J. 1989. On language death in eastern Africa. In Dorian (ed.), 13–31.

Dixon, R. M. W. 1972. *The Dyirbal language of North Queensland*. Cambridge: Cambridge University Press.

1991. The endangered languages of Australia, Indonesia and Oceania. In Robins and Uhlenbeck (eds.), 229–55.

1997. *The rise and fall of languages*. Cambridge: Cambridge University Press.

Dorian, Nancy C. 1981. *Language death: the life cycle of a Scottish Gaelic dialect*. Philadelphia: University of Pennsylvania Press.

ed. 1989. *Investigating obsolescence: studies in language contraction and death*. Cambridge: Cambridge University Press.

1993. A response to Ladefoged's other view of endangered languages. *Language* 69. 575–9.

1998. Western language ideologies and small-language prospects. In Grenoble and Whaley (eds.), 3–21.

Duffy, J. 1953. *Epidemics in Colonial America*. Baton Rouge, LA: Louisiana State University Press.

Duranti, Alessandro. 1997. *Linguistic anthropology*. Cambridge: Cambridge University Press.

Ebes, Hank, and Michael Hollow, eds. 1992. *Modern art – ancient icon*. Melbourne: The Aboriginal Gallery of Dreamings.

Eco, Umberto. 1995. *The search for the perfect language*. Oxford: Blackwell.

Edmonds, Margot, and Ella E Clark. 1989. *Voices of the winds: native American legends*. New York: Facts on File.

Edwards, John. 1985. *Language, society and identity*. Oxford: Blackwell.

1992. Sociopolitical aspects of language maintenance and loss: towards a typology of minority language situations. In Willem Fase, Koen Jaspaert, and Sjaak Kroon (eds.), *Maintenance and loss of minority languages*. Amsterdam: Benjamins, 37–54.

Edwards, V., and T. J. Sienkewicz. 1990. *Oral cultures past and present*. Oxford: Blackwell.

Eliot, T. S. 1942/53. The Classics and the man of letters. (Presidential address to the Classical Association in Cambridge, 1942.) In John Hayward (ed.), *Selected prose*. Harmondsworth: Penguin, 233–9.

Emerson, Ralph Waldo. 1833/1909. *Journals of Ralph Waldo Emerson*. Boston: Houghton Mifflin.

1844. *Essays: second series*. Boston: Phillips, Sampson.

1860. *The conduct of life*. Boston: Ticknor and Fields.

England, Nora C. 1998. Mayan efforts toward language preservation. In Grenoble and Whaley (eds.), 99–116.

European Bureau for Lesser Used Languages. 1994. *Vade-mecum: guide to legal documents, support structures and action programmes pertaining to the lesser used languages of Europe*. Dublin.

Evans, Nicholas. 1998. Aborigines speak a primitive language. In Laurie Bauer and Peter Trudgill (eds.), *Language myths*. Harmondsworth: Penguin, 159–68.

forthcoming. The last speaker is dead – long live the last speaker! In Paul Newman and Martha Ratcliff (eds), *Linguistic fieldwork*. Cambridge: Cambridge University Press.

Fill, Alwin. 1998. Ecolinguistics – state of the art 1998. *AAA – Arbeiten aus Anglistik und Amerikanistik* 23(1), 3–16.

Fill, Alwin and Peter Mülhäusler, eds. 2001. *The ecolinguistics reader*. London: Continuum.

Fishman, J. A. 1987. Language spread and language policy for endangered languages. In *Proceedings of the Georgetown University Round Table on Language and Linguistics*. Washington: Georgetown University Press, 1–15.

1991. *Reversing language shift*. Clevedon: Multilingual Matters.

Furbee, N. Louanna, Lori A. Stanley, and Tony Arkeketa. 1998. The roles of two kinds of expert in language renewal. In Ostler (ed.), 75–9.

Geary, James. 1997. Speaking in tongues. *Time* (7 July 1997), 52–8.

Gerdts, Donna B. 1998. Beyond expertise: the role of the linguist in language revitalization programs. In Ostler (ed.), 14.

Golla, Victor. 1998. Contribution to 'What language is revitalized after all?' *Ogmios* 8. 20.

Graddol, David. 1997. *The future of English*. London: The British Council.

Grenand, Pierre, and Françoise Grenand. 1993. Amérique Equatoriale: Grande Amazonie. In Serge Bahuchet (ed.), *Situation des populations indigènes des forêts denses et humides*. Luxemburg: Office des publications officielles des communautés européennes, 89–176.

Grenoble, Lenore A., and Lindsay I. Whaley, eds. 1998a. *Endangered languages: current issues and future prospects*. Cambridge: Cambridge University Press.

1998b. Toward a typology of language endangerment. In Grenoble and Whaley (1998a), 22–54.

Grimes, Barbara F., ed. 1996. *Ethnologue: languages of the world*. 13th edn. Dallas, TX: Summer Institute of Linguistics.

Grin, F. 1996. The economics of language: survey, assessment, and prospects. *International Journal of the Sociology of Language* 121. 17–44.

Grinevald, Colette. 1998. Language endangerment in South America: a programmatic approach. In Grenoble and Whaley (eds.), 124–59.

Grosjean, François. 1982. *Life with two languages*. Cambridge, MA: Harvard University Press.

Gumperz, John J., and Stephen C. Levinson, eds. 1996. *Rethinking linguistic relativity*. Cambridge: Cambridge University Press.

Hagège, Claude. 2001. *Halte à la mort des langues*. Paris: Edition Odile Jacob.

Haiman, J., and P. Benincà. 1992. *The Rhaeto-Romance languages*. London: Routledge.

Hale, Ken. 1992a. On endangered languages and the safeguarding of diversity. *Language* 68. 1–3.

1992b. Language endangerment and the human value of linguistic diversity. *Language* 68. 35–42.

1995. Contribution to a seminar on Endangered Languages, Dartmouth College, Hanover (New Hampshire, USA). *Iatiku* 1. 5.

1998. On endangered languages and the importance of linguistic diversity. In Grenoble and Whaley (eds.), 205 ff.

Harrison, B. 1997. Language integration: results of an intergenerational analysis. *Statistical Journal of the United Nations ECE* 14. 289–303.

Haugen, Einar. 1971. The ecology of language. *Linguistic Reporter*, Supplement 25 to vol. 13 (1). 25.

1972. *The ecology of language*. Stanford: Stanford University Press.

Heidegger, Martin. 1971. *On the way to language*, translated by P. D. Hertz. New York: Harper and Row.

Henze, Hans Werner. 1982. *Music and politics: collected writings 1953–81*, translated by Peter Labanyi. London: Faber.

Hockett, Charles F. 1958. *A course in modern linguistics*. New York: Macmillan.

Hoenigswald, Henry M. 1989. Language obsolescence and language history: matters of linearity, leveling, loss, and the like. In Dorian (ed.), 347–54.

Holloway, Charles E. 1997. *Dialect death: the case of Brule Spanish*. Amsterdam: Benjamins.

Holmes, Oliver Wendell, Sr. 1860. *The professor at the breakfast table*. Boston: Ticknor and Fields.

Holt, Dennis. 1998. may·por·é: a linguistic sculpture. *Endangered Language Fund Newsletter* 2 (1). 1–3.

Hook, Brian, ed. 1982. *The Cambridge encyclopedia of China*. Cambridge: Cambridge University Press.

Hornberger, Nancy, and Kendall King. 1996. Contribution to a conference on Authenticity and Identity in Indigenous Language Revitalization (American Anthropological Association), held in November 1996. *Newsletter of the Foundation for Endangered Languages* 5. 19.

Hughes, Geoffrey. 1988. *Words in time.* Oxford: Blackwell.

Hymes, Dell. 1966. *Introduction to Part 2 of Language in culture and society.* New York: Harper and Row.

Iorwerth, Dylan. 1995. *A week in Europe.* Cardiff: University of Wales Press.

Ivanov, Vjaceslav. 1992. Reconstructing the past. *Intercom* 15 (1).

Jacobs, Kaia'titahkhe Annette. 1998. A chronology of Mohawk language instruction at Kahnawà:ke. In Grenoble and Whaley (eds.), 117–23.

Jahn, Jens-Eberhard. 1998. Minority languages in Istria: experiences from a sociolinguistic fieldwork. In Ostler (ed.), 45–52.

James, Carl. 1977. Welsh bilingualism – fact and fiction. *Language Problems and Language Planning* 1. 73–81.

1999. Language awareness: implications for the language curriculum. *Language, Culture, Curriculum* 12. 94–115.

Jocks, Christopher. 1998. Living words and cartoon translations: long-house 'texts' and the limitations of English. In Grenoble and Whaley (eds.), 217–33.

Johnson, Jerald Jay. 1978. Yana. In R. F. Heizer (ed.), *Handbook of North American Indians*, vol. viii. Washington: Smithsonian Institution 361–9.

Johnson, Samuel. 1990 (1773). *A journey to the Western Islands of Scotland.* Harmondsworth: Penguin.

Jones, Ann E. 1985. Erydiad geirfaol ym Mhenterfi Clunderwen, Efailwen a Llandysilio (Lexical erosion in the villages of Clunderwen, Efailwen and Llandysilio). *Cardiff Working Papers in Welsh Linguistics* 4. 81–100.

Jones, Steve, Robert Martin, and David Pilbeam, eds. 1992. *The Cambridge encyclopedia of human evolution.* Cambridge: Cambridge University Press.

Kaufman, Terrence. 1994. The native languages of South America. In Christopher Moseley and R. E. Asher (eds.), *Atlas of the world's languages*. London: Routledge, 46–76.

Kellett, Arnold. 1996. *Ee by gum, Lord! The Gospels in broad Yorkshire*. Otley: Smith Settle.

Kincade, M. Dale. 1991. The decline of native languages in Canada. In Robins and Uhlenbeck (eds.), 157–76.

Kipling, Rudyard. 1912/28. The uses of reading. (Speech at Wellington College, 1912.) In Rudyard Kipling, *A book of words*. Doubleday: Doran, 73–90.

Koch, Eddie, and Siven Maslamoney. 1997. Words that click and rustle softly like the wild. *Mail & Guardian* (Braamfontein), 12–18 September 1997, 28.

Krauss, Michael. 1992. The world's languages in crisis. *Language* 68. 4–10.

1998. The scope of the language endangerment crisis and recent response to it. In Matsumura (ed.), 108–9.

Kroskrity, Paul V. 1993. *Language, history and identity: ethnolinguistic studies of the Arizona Tewa*. Tucson: University of Arizona Press.

Ladefoged, Peter. 1992. Another view of endangered languages. *Language* 68. 809–11.

Landaburu, Jon. 1979. *La langue des Andoke* (Amazonie colombienne), Paris: SELAF.

Landweer, M. Lynn. 1998. Indicators of ethnolinguistic vitality: case study of two languages – Labu and Vanimo. In Ostler (ed.), 64–72.

Langgaard, Per. 1992. Greenlandic is not an ideology, it is a language. In N. H. H. Graburn and R. Iutzi-Mitchell (eds.), *Language and educational policy in the north*. Berkeley: University of California, 167–78.

Lord, A. B. 1960. *The singer of tales*. Cambridge, MA: Harvard University Press.

McArthur, Tom. 1998. *The English languages*. Cambridge: Cambridge University Press.

McDaniel, Matthew. 1998. The Akha Heritage Foundation. *Ogmios* 7. 14–15.

MacDougall, R. C. 1998. Individuals, cultures and telecommunication technology. In Ostler (ed.), 91–8.

McKay, Graham. 1996. Comment. *Iatiku* 2. 18–19.

McNeill, W. H. 1976. *Plagues and peoples*. Garden City, NY: Anchor Press.

Maddieson, Ian. 1984. *Patterns of sounds*. Cambridge: Cambridge University Press.

Maguire, Gabrielle. 1991. *Our own language: an Irish initiative*. Clevedon: Multilingual Matters.

Malouf, David. 1985. The only speaker of his tongue. In *Antipodes: stories*. Sydney: Random House.

Markey, Thomas L. 1988. Ladin and other relic language forms in the eastern Alpine region. In Jacek Fisiak (ed.), *Historical dialectology: regional and social*. Berlin: Mouton de Gruyter, 357–75.

Martin, Laura. 1986. 'Eskimo words for snow': a case study in the genesis and decay of an anthropological sample. *American Anthropologist* 88. 418–23.

Maslow, Abraham. 1954. *Motivation and personality*. New York: Harper and Row.

Matisoff, James A. 1991. Endangered languages of Mainland Southeast Asia. In Robins and Uhlenbeck (eds.), 189–228.

Matsumura, Kazuto, ed. 1998. *Studies in endangered languages* (Papers from the International Symposium on Endangered Languages, Tokyo, 18–20 November 1995.) Tokyo: Hituzi Syobo.

Maurais, J., ed. 1996. *Quebec's aboriginal languages: history, planning and development*. Clevedon: Multilingual Matters.

Menn, Lise. 1989. Some people who don't talk right: universal and particular in child language, aphasia, and language obsolescence. In Dorian (ed.), 335–45.

Mikhalchenko, V. Y. 1998. Endangered languages of Russia: an informational database. In Matsumura (ed.), 129–38.

Mithun, Marianne. 1998. The significance of diversity in language endangerment and preservation. In Grenoble and Whaley (eds.), 163–91.

Mosely, Christopher, and R. E. Asher, eds. 1994. *Atlas of the world's languages*. London: Routledge.

Mühlhäusler, Peter. 1990. 'Reducing' Pacific languages to writing. In J. E. Joseph and T. J. Taylor (eds.), *Ideologies of language*. London: Routledge, 189–205.

1995. *Linguistic ecology: language change and linguistic imperialism in the Pacific rim*. London: Routledge.

Nettle, Daniel and Suzanne Romaine. 2001. *Vanishing voices*. Oxford: Oxford University Press.

Ngugi wa Thiong'o. 1986. *Decolonising the mind: the politics of language in African literature*. London: Currey / Portsmouth, NH: Heinemann.

Norris, Mary Jane. 1998. Canada's aboriginal languages. *Canadian Social Trends*, Winter.

Odum, Eugene P. 1986. Ecosystems. *Encyclopaedia Britannica*. 15th edn. Macropaedia XVII, 979–83.

Ostler, Nicholas. 1996. Tongues ancient and postmodern. *Iatiku* 3. 1–2.

1997. Editorial. *Ogmios* 6. 3–5.

ed. 1998. *Endangered languages: what role for the specialist?* (Proceedings of the Second FEL Conference, University of Edinburgh, 25–7 September 1998.) Bath: Foundation for Endangered Languages.

Pagel, Mark. 1995. Contribution to the Conservation of Endangered Languages seminar, University of Bristol, 21 April 1995. *Iatiku* 1. 6.

Palmer, F. R. 1986. *Mood and modality*. Cambridge: Cambridge University Press.

Paul, D. A. 1973. *The Navajo code talkers*. Pittsburgh, PA: Dorrance.

Peat, F. David. 1995. *Blackfoot physics*. London: Fourth Estate.

Pei, Mario. 1952. *The story of language*. London: Allen and Unwin.

1954. *All about language*. Philadelphia: Lippincott.

Pinter, Harold. 1988. *Mountain language*. London: Faber.

Pogson, Geoff. 1998. Digital technology will save your language. *InfoNT* 2 (Conférence des Services de Traduction des Etats Européens, The Hague), 1–5.

Posey, Darrell. 1997. Biological and cultural diversity – the inextricable linked by language and politics. Summary in *Iatiku* 4. 7–8.

Pound, Ezra. 1960. *The ABC of reading*. New York: Laughlin.

Price, Glanville, ed. 1998. *Encyclopedia of the languages of Europe*. Oxford: Blackwell.

Pullum, G. K. 1991. *The great Eskimo vocabulary hoax*. Chicago: Chicago University Press.

Quesada, J. Diego. 1998. Competing interpretations of history: what if they are wrong? In Ostler (ed.), 53–7.

Reyhner, Jon, ed. 1997. *Teaching indigenous languages*. Flagstaff: Northern Arizona University.

Rhydwen, Mari. 1998. Strategies for doing the impossible. In Ostler (ed.), 101–6.

Robins, R. H., and E. M. Uhlenbeck, eds. 1991. *Endangered languages*. Oxford and New York: Berg.

Rodrigues, A. D. 1993. Linguas indígenas: 500 anos de descobertas e perdas. *DELTA* 9. 83–103.

Romaine, Suzanne. 1989. Pidgins, creoles, immigrant, and dying languages. In Dorian (ed.), 369–83.

Rosen, Barbara. 1994. Is English really a family of languages? *International Herald Tribune*, 15 October.

Rubin, Joan. 1985. Toward bilingual education in Paraguay. In J. E. Alatis and J. J. Staczek (eds.), *Perspectives on bilingualism and bilingual education*. Washington: Georgetown University Press, 423–35.

Ruhlen, Merritt. 1987. *A guide to the world's languages*. Stanford: Stanford University Press.

Sapir, Edward. 1921. *Language*. New York: Harcourt, Brace, and World.

Sawai, Harumi. 1998. The present situation of the Ainu language. In Matsumura (ed.), 177–89.

Schiller, Herbert I. 1969. *Mass communications and American empire*. New York: Kelley.

1976. *Communication and cultural domination*. New York: Sharpe.

Sealey, Alison. 1996. *Learning about language: issues for primary teachers*. Buckingham: Open University Press.

Seifart, Frank. 1998. Situation of the indigenous languages of Colombia, especially Chimila. *Ogmios* 9. 8–10.

Silverstein, M., ed. 1971. *Whitney on language*. Cambridge, MA: MIT Press.

Skutnabb-Kangas, Tove. 1996. Comment. *Iatiku* 3. 8.

Sloboda, John A. 1986. *The musical mind: the cognitive psychology of music*. Oxford: Oxford University Press.

Stearn, E. W., and A. E. Stearn. 1945. *The effect of smallpox on the destiny of the Amerindian*. Boston: Humphries.

Steiner, George. 1967. *Language and silence*. London: Faber and Faber.

Swann, B., ed. 1992. *On the translation of Native American literatures*. Washington: Smithsonian Institution Press.

Thomas, Lewis. 1980. On meddling. In *The medusa and the snail: more notes of a biology watcher*. London: Allen Lane.

Todd, Loreto. 1984. *Modern Englishes: pidgins and creoles*. Oxford: Blackwell.

Tosco, Mauro. 1997. Contribution to a symposium on Endangered Languages in Africa, Leipzig. *Ogmios* 6. 21.

Trosterud, Trond. 1997. On supporting threatened languages. *Iatiku* 4. 22–4.

1999. How many written languages in the world? *Ogmios* 11. 16–18.

Trudgill, Peter. 1991. Language maintenance and language shift: preservation versus extinction. *International Journal of Applied Linguistics* 1. 61–9.

2000. *Sociolinguistics*. 4th edn. Harmondsworth: Penguin.

Valiquette, Hilaire Paul. 1998. Community, professionals, and language preservation: first things first. In Ostler (ed.), 107–12.

References

Van Deusen-Scholl, Nelleke. 1998. Heritage language instruction: issues and challenges. *AILA News* 1. 12–14.

Van Hoorde, Johan. 1998. Let Dutch die? Over the Taalunie's dead body. *InfoNT* 2 (Conférence des Services de Traduction des Etats Européens, The Hague), 6–10.

Voegelin, C. F., and F. M. Voegelin. 1977. *Classification and index of the world's languages.* New York: Elsevier.

Vydrine, Valentin. 1998. Kagoro: a language transforming into a dialect? *Ogmios* 8. 3–5.

Walker, Ronald. 1993. Language shift in Europe and Irian Jaya, Indonesia: toward the heart of the matter. *AILA Review* 10. 77–87.

Wardhaugh, Ronald. 1987. *Languages in competition.* Oxford: Blackwell.

Watson, Seosamh. 1991. Scottish and Irish Gaelic: the giants' bed-fellows. In Robins and Uhlenbeck (eds.), 41–59.

Weinreich, Max. 1980. *History of the Yiddish language.* Chicago: University of Chicago Press.

Whatmough, Joshua. 1956. *Language: a modern synthesis.* London: Secker and Warburg.

Wheeler, Rebecca, ed. 1999. *The workings of language.* New York: Praeger.

Woodbury, Anthony C. 1998. Documenting rhetorical, aesthetic, and expressive loss in language shift. In Grenoble and Whaley (eds.), 234–58.

Wurm, Stephen A. 1991. Language death and disappearance: causes and circumstances. In Robins and Uhlenbeck (eds.), 1–18.

1998. Methods of language maintenance and revival, with selected cases of language endangerment in the world. In Matsumura (ed.), 191–211.

Wyman, Thornton. 1996. Contribution to a conference on Authenticity and Identity in Indigenous Language Revitalization (American Anthropological Association), held in November 1996. *Newsletter of the Foundation for Endangered Languages* 5. 20.

239

Yallop, Colin. 1982. *Australian aboriginal languages*. London: Deutsch.

Yamamoto, Akira Y. 1997. A survey of endangered languages and related resources. *Newsletter of the Foundation for Endangered Languages* 5. 8–14.

1998a. Linguists and endangered language communities: issues and approaches. In Matsumura (ed.), 213–52.

1998b. Retrospect and prospect on new emerging language communities. In Ostler (ed.), 114.

INDEX OF DIALECTS, LANGUAGES, LANGUAGE FAMILIES, AND ETHNIC GROUPS

INDEX OF AUTHORS AND SPEAKERS

SUBJECT INDEX

The alphabetical order of this index is word-by-word.

indifference to indigenous
   languages 109
indigenous, as a label 68
Indo-European 72, 203
Indonesia 5, 6
industries 40, 176
inflections 29
informants *see* consultants
information
   gathering 4, 12, 122
   technology 189
inheritance 50
Institute for the Preservation of
   the Original Languages of
   the Americas 222
intellectual rights 210
intelligibility
   distinguishing language and
      dialect 10, 12
   vs. identity 38
intergenerational transmission
   26, 187
International Clearing House for
   Endangered Languages vii,
   122, 222
international collaboration 132
*International encyclopedia of
   linguistics* 4
*International Journal of the
   Sociology of Language* 40
international languages 156
International Linguistics
   Congress vii
International PEN Club 121
internationalization 190
Internet 132, 189, 190
interpreting 174
   cost of 39
intervention issues 37, 123, 142,
   143, 149, 169, 204, 208, 219
invisibility of language 109, 110
Ireland 112
Irian Jaya 6

Irish potato famine 93
isolated languages 27, 72, 203
Israel 170
IT *see* information, technology
Italy 176, 177, 199

Japan 112, 172

kinship 81, 82, 83, 84, 201,
   204, 209
knowledge
   expressed by language 62
   management 190
   systematized by encyclopedias
      146
kohanga reo 171

Lancashire dialect 48
Language 44
language
   as barrier to communication
      36, 45
   attitudes 25, 59, 88, 104, 105,
      106, 107, 109, 110, 112, 114,
      117, 123, 129, 132, 136, 142,
      147, 153, 156, 215
   awareness 29, 34, 121, 127,
      143, 144, 182, 183, 203, 216
   change 90
   classification 27, 125, 203
   committees 155
   conflict 36, 38
   contact 92, 130
   discovery 5, 6
   distribution 6, 192
   dominance 101
   extremists 153, 167
   faculty in humans 14, 68,
      71, 84
   interest 15, 46, 95, 123, 127,
      132, 137, 194
   learning 130, 204, 206
   loyalty 22, 180

Printed in the United States
By Bookmasters